Patricia Zukowski, Editor

The Anthology Editorial Board:
Anne Bello
Shastri Akella
Hazel Gedikli
Rebecca Griffin
Elizabeth Mikesch
Anna Klebanowska Piecuch
Ann Ward

The Student Writing Anthology

2016–2017

University of Massachusetts Amherst

Writing Program

macmillan learning
curriculum solutions

bedford/st.martin's · hayden-mcneil · w.h. freeman · worth publishers

ISBN 978-0-7380-8437-4

Macmillan Learning Curriculum Solutions
14903 Pilot Drive
Plymouth, MI 48170
www.macmillanlearning.com

Hoang 8437-4 F16

Hayden-McNeil Sustainability

Hayden-McNeil's standard paper stock uses a minimum of 30% post-consumer waste. We offer higher % options by request, including a 100% recycled stock. Additionally, Hayden-McNeil Custom Digital provides authors with the opportunity to convert print products to a digital format. Hayden-McNeil is part of a larger sustainability initiative through Macmillan Learning. Visit http://sustainability.macmillan.com to learn more.

Table of Contents

Part 1: Essays from *Basic Writing*

Part 2: Writing from and across Contexts: Essays from *College Writing*

Writer's Statement

Introduction

Since 1982, the Writing Program has worked from the core belief that undergraduate students are immersed in a rich print and digital culture and that they are *already writers* whose ideas are worth sharing, crafting, and revising into prose that should be read. This 39th edition of the UMass Amherst *Student Writing Anthology* maintains our longstanding respect for student writing by publishing select essays written for first-year writing classes in the fall and spring of the 2014–2015 academic year. The book serves as an essential learning and teaching tool in both our *Basic* and *College Writing* courses, praised and prized for its value by students and teachers alike. It also fulfills the critical goal of helping these texts to circulate among a wider readership.

We invite you to contemplate the vital issues and original thinking in these essays, and for those who are reading *as writers,* to also consider the effects of each author's rhetorical choices. Part 1 begins with essays selected from *Basic Writing*—a reading- and writing-intensive course that explores issues of U.S. diversity. Its students read and write about physical, national, linguistic, and cultural borders that shape life in the United States. The excellent writing from this course asks us to consider how culture and identity interact—reinforcing some borders and blurring others. Understanding how societies differ and valuing cultural difference—including different forms of communication—are essential educational experiences for us all. Our Deputy Director and head of our *Basic Writing* course, Anne Bello, provides a far richer and more detailed explanation of the course in her preface to the *Basic Writing* section of this book.

Part 2, devoted to *College Writing*, illustrates the goals of that course: to write with purpose and power, to develop one's ideas critically, and to effectively tailor one's prose to a specific audience. In this course, students are asked to explore topics that are personally meaningful and to write about these topics to readers who *need* to engage with these ideas. In these essays, readers will find that students are not only writing to our university community, but also translating the thinking and research valued in the academy to a broader public. This section begins with essays from three of the course's five units: "Inquiring into Self," "Interacting with Text," and "Adding to the Conversation." Our fourth unit is called the "TBA" because each of our teachers designs a unique project. While these assignments build on goals and concepts covered in the first three units of the course, we have not included essays from this unit since each project is specific to each class. The section concludes with the final essay assignment, the "Writer's Statement." Throughout the course, students reflect on various aspects of their drafting, revision process, and the final product of their work. In the "Writer's Statement," students look back over the whole body of work they have produced in the course, consider their struggles and successes, then synthesize into one paper what they believe are the most salient lessons they will carry with them from the course. These papers offer sound and insightful advice to any writer.

We welcome readers to discover the many rhetorical choices available to us in academic writing and to learn from the wealth of ideas and experiences that emerge from each writer's personal context. Finally, we hope our readers will enjoy the excellent work produced by UMass Amherst students.

Acknowledgments

This seemingly small book represents an enormous amount of commitment, support, and hard work from so many people, and I am grateful to them all: the First Year Writing instructors who nominated their students' excellent texts for possible inclusion in the *Anthology* (far too many names to recognize here), and all the students who so eagerly agreed to share their work so that others might learn from it. But not even the first step of creating this book could have gone forward without the extremely professional and dedicated work of my editorial assistant, Ann Ward. A graduate student in our MFA program, Ann's work was key, and all of her efforts exceeded my expectations. From logging in submissions, organizing essays for the committee to read, creating and updating master score sheets, attending and taking notes of all committee meetings to being my second reader in editing the book—and so much more—her assistance was invaluable to me, and I am filled with gratitude. Our new publisher, Hayden-McNeil, also deserves recognition for their conscientious support and quick responses to urgent problems that arose, including circulation issues with a new university textbook distributor and chasing down the creator of our cover image to avoid concerns expressed by their legal department.

*****

The efforts of our *College Writing* Anthology Committee members were remarkable. Every week throughout the fall 2015 semester, each member received a batch of 15–20 papers, read them intensively and attentively, then scored and commented on each one. The committee met Friday afternoons to thoughtfully, thoroughly, and spiritedly discuss each text being considered that week. Five volunteer graduate student members, Shastri Akella, Hazel Gedikli, Rebecca Griffin, Elizabeth Mikesch, and Anna Klebanowska Piecuch showed graciousness and dedication throughout the entire process. I am particularly indebted to them for their valuable contributions to my introductions to the *College Writing* essays. We were also privileged to have Anne Bello, Deputy Director of the Writing Program, participate as a full committee member at every meeting. The work she contributed was critical in creating the final book. Not only did she serve on the Anthology Committee, offering rich insights into *College Writing* submissions; she also was responsible for creating the entire *Basic Writing* section. With graduate student instructors Joshua Barsczewski and Kelin Loe, Anne selected the essays that appear in the *Basic Writing* section. She also edited all of the *Basic Writing* essays, formatted the section, and composed a highly instructive preface. I would be remiss to not thank members of our office staff, Heidi Terault and Becky Blajda, for their considerable contributions to many aspects of the book, particularly getting the book into the hands of our student authors, program instructors, and incoming freshman. Finally, I am grateful to Writing Program Director Haivan Hoang—for her enthusiastic support of this project, her patient and sound advice on so many matters, and the critical ways she supported me personally during her tenure as director. Through these efforts of so many dedicated members of the Writing Program, all of our first-year students and teachers will have access to this valuable learning resource—a required text in both *Basic* and *College Writing*.

Patricia Zukowski
Chair, Anthology Committee

Part 1

Essays from *Basic Writing*

Preface

ANNE BELLO

Turn on the news, and borders seem to be everywhere, from political debates about immigration to stories of migrants fleeing conflict and seeking economic opportunity. But as the essays in this collection show, borders are not just national and physical: they can be intangible markers of difference; they can be seemingly impenetrable barriers to change; and they can be crossed, sometimes easily, sometimes at great cost.

Students in *Basic Writing* spend the semester writing and reading about borders, their many forms, and their often complex implications. Throughout the semester, students work through four main units: Colliding Spaces, which examines physical, spatial, and geographical borders as well as intangible borders; Defining Lines, where the focus shifts to national borders and questions of immigration and assimilation; Interweavings, which considers how culture and identity shape and are shaped by borders; and Unsettled Voices, which explores how language crosses, creates, and challenges borders. As students progress through these units, they produce essays that engage with readings and course content in a variety of ways, experimenting with different writing "moves": writing from personal experience; entering into a dialogue with a reading; analyzing a text; and using multiple sources to persuade readers. *Basic Writing* instructors decide which sequences of units and writing moves are the best fit for their classes; during the first unit of the course, one section might be analyzing a text focused on the theme of language, while another section might be writing from personal experience about physical borders. By the end of the semester, all *Basic Writing* students consider the same thematic units and explore the same writing moves, but each class follows a different path to that end.

As a result, the essays in this section do not correspond to specific units the way the essays in the *College Writing* section do. Instead, these essays show a range of possible ways for students to write about—and alongside, in response to, and even against—other texts in the course. For example, Shuai Gu's and José Reyes' essays bear many similarities to each other on the

3

surface level: both authors incorporate personal experience and interact with two published texts in essays about language. Gu, however, uses personal experience to add to Fan Shen's and Maxine Hong Kingston's observations about linguistic and cultural differences between China and the United States. Reyes, on the other hand, draws on his personal experience along with Kingston's and Amy Tan's essays to argue for reform to language education in the United States. Gu writes with Shen and Kingston; Reyes uses Tan and Kingston to persuade readers. Likewise, Sara MacDonald and Wei Wei both write about Bharati Mukherjee's "Two Ways to Belong in America" in their essays. MacDonald incorporates Mukherjee's experience as she reflects upon how different members of her family have related to their Armenian heritage. Wei, looking at a similar passage from Mukherjee's essay, raises questions about the meaning of the term "pure culture" in her consideration of how studying abroad poses questions about assimilation.

Some of the essays in this section do lend themselves to particular units and particular genres. Aneeswar Bairavasundaram's essay, for instance, is a rhetorical analysis of an essay that speaks directly to the themes of the Unsettled Voices unit. Jessica Mazzola writes directly from personal experience in an essay that fits most neatly with the Colliding Spaces unit, and Anna Capobianco sets up a dialogue with Leslie Feinberg's "We Are All Works in Progress." Before each essay is a short introduction, which suggests how the text might fit into the *Basic Writing* curriculum. These introductions, however, are not meant to limit how these essays might be taken up in the *Basic Writing* classroom. Bairavasundaram's attention to Baldwin's diction provides an interesting example of close reading, while Mazzola's essay shows how personal reflection can be used to complicate course concepts. Capobianco's essay demonstrates one way writers can experiment with structure. In short, these essays are not meant to be confined within the borders of a particular unit.

These essays do, however, provide content for students to respond *to*. Oshiomah Oyageshio, who uses multiple sources as well as personal experience to persuade readers, ends his essay by asking, "Racism is not dead. Will it ever be?" In her conclusion, Merveille Kazimoto challenges readers to envision "an America where living bilingually, multi-culturally, and transnationally is acceptable and not anything 'alien.'" These essays highlight complicated issues and pose difficult questions, pointing to the challenging intellectual work of the course. Just as students in *Basic Writing* are encouraged to write in dialogue with James Baldwin and Amy Tan, they are also invited to engage with the ideas of Oyageshio and Kazimoto, of Bairavasundaram, Capobianco, Gu, MacDonald, Mazzola, Reyes, and Wei.

Rhetorical Analysis of Baldwin's "If Black English Isn't a Language, Then Tell Me, What Is?"

ANEESWAR BAIRAVASUNDARAM

In this textual analysis, Bairavasundaram examines how James Baldwin's tone and word choice create pathos and logos. Pathos and logos are two ways writers can persuade or influence readers. When using pathos, writers appeal to readers' emotions; when using logos, writers use logic, knowledge, and facts to influence readers' responses. Bairavasundaram analyzes how Baldwin's choices as a writer support his argument in favor of Black English.

"*A language comes into existence by means of brutal necessity*" (Baldwin 154–155).

Black English, a language with a majority of Black speakers, represents the dark and oppressive historical past of the United States. In 1979, a prominent figure, James Baldwin, addressed the importance of classifying Black English as a new language and the historic relevance of the language's formation. In his essay, Baldwin also criticizes the ignorant attitude towards Black English and its consequence on the Black community. He ultimately pushes for classifying Black English as a language, which is an important step for social equality.

Baldwin uses aspects of emotion portraying anger when describing a reason why Black English is not considered a language. Baldwin states the white people's dilemma of not being able to "afford to understand [Black English]. This understanding would reveal to [them] too much about [themselves] and smash that mirror before which [they have] been frozen for so long" (155). By stating that white people cannot accept their historic past and Black English's history, he claims that calling Black English a dialect of English is a manner to circumvent the dark past of the United States. In context of the Civil Rights movement, Baldwin suggests that the reason behind the lack of racial equality stems from white peoples' inability to bear their slave-owning past and accept how they are truly viewed in an oppressive view by Blacks.

Baldwin shows his true emotion when describing the white people who disrespect Black English as "*uptight*, middle-class white people, imitating poverty, trying to *get down*" (154). Baldwin's voice dramatically changes from a neutral tone into an angry and serious tone when he mentions white people using but not respecting the Black language, which in turn disrespects the Black culture. The shift of tone signifies what impact white people's ignorance of the Black culture has on Blacks. He indicates that white people do not understand that imitating poverty is much different than true poverty and tries to state that certain terms and phrases have a much deeper meaning (154). He also uses Black language when describing white people's actions such as "trying to *get down*." By using "Black" terms he assures both his knowledge of the language as well as uses it as a means of giving the true definition of the "Black" terms. In addition, many literary rules applying to foreign languages are used. For example, he writes that it is "late in the day to attempt to penalize black people for having created a language that permits the nation its only glimpse of reality … without which the nation would be even more *whipped* than it is" (154). Baldwin uses sarcasm to explain that Black English's origin stems from the times of slavery and explains how the language symbolizes the United States' dark past. He italicized "*whipped*" to denote the word as if he were including words from another language. The placement of the term from Black English is carefully chosen as it is after Baldwin uses his logos to explain why Black English is a language. By doing so Baldwin slowly causes the readers to go through a logical process and accept Black English as a separate language.

In addition to conveying his emotion to his readers, Baldwin also uses logical statements to enforce his thesis on his target audience. As Baldwin begins to state that Black English should be considered its own language, he begins by making a series of arguments which eventually end by proving his point. Baldwin states that the status of language "has nothing to do with language itself but with the role of language" (153). Baldwin begins by stating the argument that he is trying to prove of what role language plays and how Black English fulfills the roles of a language. Baldwin states facts about Black history and defines language as "[coming] into existence by means of brutal necessity" (154–155). By giving historical facts of Black English's existence, Baldwin lets readers discern whether Black English fulfills the criteria of a language. He also describes the role of language and how it "reveals the private identity [of an individual]" (153), so that to "open your mouth … is (if I may use black English) to 'put your business in the street'" (154). The role of language is described as a marker of identity. Baldwin carefully uses terms from Black English to give an example of how language serves as a classification of identity as well as to cause the readers to relate with personal experiences in dealing with others who speak foreign languages.

Baldwin using logos and pathos causes the reader to accept that Black English is a separate language. Baldwin indicates that when white people ignorantly mock Black English and use disrespectful terms, they are insulting a culture that had gone through decades of being oppressed. Through his sudden anger and shift in tone, Baldwin emphasizes the need for change. Being written post-Civil Rights era shows that political equality is not sufficient enough but also that societal equality is equally as important. Baldwin's overarching concept is that no language or dialect should be made fun of as each language represents a culture and each culture represents the struggles and happiness of a community.

Work Cited

Baldwin, James. "If Black English Isn't a Language, Then Tell Me, What Is?" *Reading and Writing on the Edge.* Eds. Deirdre Vinyard et al. Boston: Pearson, 2014. 152–155. Print. Mercury Reader Ser.

Because I'm a Girl

ANNA CAPOBIANCO

Using quotations from Leslie Feinberg's "We Are All Works in Progress" as a starting point, Capobianco writes from personal experience, reflecting on how gender has functioned as a border in her life. Capobianco balances narrative and detail with critical reflection on her personal experiences.

"I actually chafe at describing myself as masculine. For one thing, masculinity is such an expansive territory, encompassing boundaries of nationality, race, and class. Most importantly, individuals blaze their own trails across this landscape" (*Feinberg 104*).

When I say I am studying to become a horticulturalist to new people, I usually get a puzzled look. They don't really know what that means or what I do for job. But once I go into detail for them describing that I work with plants and landscapers and that I garden for a living, I get some mixed reviews. My audience instantly knows that it is a male-dominated job and that it can be labor-intensive work. Some people are impressed or in awe of what I do and that makes me feel great about what I do. Then comes the criticism, which has remarks like, "You are too pretty for that" or "You don't look strong enough." I often get looks while out to lunch with my crew of guys. Proper women usually stare or make comments along the lines as, "She's one of the boys" or "She does a man's job," all of which I am not sure to take as a compliment or an offense. However, I love that I have become a marker of difference through my career, and I am proud of the young horticulturalist I am becoming. But because I am a girl, they often look at the fact that I am girl rather than my talent and knowledge with plants. There is one instance in my life that has left a mark on me and helped me shape who I am today.

"You've balked at the idea that being a woman means having to be thin as a rail, emotionally nurturing, and an airhead when it comes to balancing her checkbook. You know in your guts that being a man has nothing to do with rippling muscles, innate courage, or knowing how to handle a chain saw" (*Feinberg 100*).

The hallway was perfumed with the scent of cigarettes, and the conversations consisted of comparing scars on hands and arms. These scars were idolized like battle wounds from chain saws and tools from past jobs. Even though these stories were distractions, deep down the focus was on the interview. The lineup was all men with a few other girls other than myself. I was one of the many students to be applying for a prestigious internship. The application was open to all plant science majors, but most of the applications came from Arboriculture and Landscape students. I was the only Florist/Horticulture major in this large crowd. My hands did not bear the result of hard labor around me but instead had red polish on my nails and some of my finest jewelry on my wrist. I was well rehearsed once I entered the conference room. For weeks I was practicing saying the correct answers to each question I was asked. I sat across from the panel of employers, the dean of my program, and one teacher, who was in charge of the intern selection process. Across the panel I could see smiles and nods to my answers, all except from this one teacher. He put his head down and started messing around with the pen and paper in front of him on the desk. It puzzled me because he was so supportive of me applying beforehand, and he was so interested until this point, it seemed.

"Bigotry exacts its toll in flesh and blood. And left unchecked and unchallenged, prejudices create a poisonous climate for us all. Each of us has a stake in the demand that every human being has a right to a job, to shelter, to health care, to dignity, to respect"(Feinberg 100).

As the weeks passed the vibe shifted into a different direction. All of those students who had class with this one teacher from the panel were confident of getting the internship. I, however, was not confident at all. Then the letter of rejection came. In my head I played the interview over and over, and I still couldn't have thought of anything that would have made me deserve this letter. I spoke to my teacher the next day, and his answer has stuck with me to this day. He said, "There was nothing you could have done to change this outcome. There was one thing that you said that made you not eligible for the position. Also because of your interest here I don't think you are ready. Lastly, it is very hard to tell if you are actually interested in the industry." I was in shock because I was turned away, but who was he to decide my interest? I felt as though I never got a fair chance. What did I say to not let me get an acceptance letter? What on earth does that even mean, because I am a girl that looks her best for the interview of a lifetime for the position she so desperately wanted? It didn't seem right because I felt equal to all of those who were selected, even though I was much more professional and was working towards more experience. How was he to say I would not make it in this career? I felt my blood begin to boil and my head cloud with so many emotions. I fought for a change of the already set picks, and I got nowhere. Some girls that also stood in the lineup with me were among those selected for this opportunity. I went back to my teacher at another time to ask why the other girls were picked over me. His answer to this new question was, "Well, they have more experience and have the right look and fit for the job requirement." In that moment I knew something had to change. The passion I started to taste because of my school was quickly turning sour. I couldn't let that happen; I wasn't going to let this missed out opportunity get the best of me. The rest of my high school days were different. I pushed myself harder to make networks on my own and apply for bigger jobs and internships. When applying to college, the teacher who helped in my rejection a year and half before came back around again to help me. I politely declined: I didn't need help from someone who was so discouraging, even if he was a well-recognized alumnus from UMass. I made a name for myself in this industry; I attend college now for my passion. I can't say the same for the crew that was chosen for that prestigious internship. Turned out that some of my teacher's favorite students who he thought were better than me had failed him in the end.

Over the years I have seen more makers of difference like myself. Because most of the plant industry has to do with networking, there are many conferences and trainings throughout New England. Each time I attend one of these events the presence of women can be very low. Men do dominate the crowd, and booths and salesmen do their best to attract potential buyers as much as they can. There are some women that sell products and then there are those that just work the booths of the vendors. They have become more of a selling tool rather than appreciated as a respected member of this industry. Recently, I attended a conference where high school students were welcomed. I couldn't help but laugh because I remember my days coming to the same conference and filling my free tote bags with pamphlets and samples. But I noticed that the new generation of potential women in this industry were getting ignored at these booths by male vendors. It was discouraging to see this as they were not taken seriously. However, when I approached the same booths, I was recognized and a conversation was then sparked. I realized that things have come full circle as I now had the right look, as I was in my company's uniform. The high schoolers were dressed casually and were noticeably younger than I was. I feel because of this kind of behavior it is playing a role in the low numbers of women interested in the green industry. I can only hope that those young women that I saw soon realize that the green industry is very welcoming and that there are a lot of great opportunities. We just can't let the bad apples spoil the bunch.

"And what degree of gender expression is considered 'acceptable' can depend on your social situation, your race and nationality, your class, and whether you live in an urban or rural environment" (Feinberg 104–105).

Even though I have come a long way since my high school days, I still overcome my differences among my peers every quite often on this journey we call a career. Employers are now seeing that I am much more than my given gender, and I have grown in experience. At times I am hired over some men that are also applying for the same job. But then there are also times where I do miss out on an opportunity where men are strictly preferred for the job. I strive to do better and to succeed in my career, however, and I don't let these missed chances determine my outcome. Letting these markers separate myself from others is diminishing as I continue to establish my name and reputation in my passion. I wish it could be this way for so many other women in this industry, as some are just starting out and trying to find their place. The times are surely changing, and I think over time women will finally become more than something to come home to after a long day of landscaping. But rather a colleague with you during that long day, creating beautiful gardens, operating equipment, and learning alongside one another.

Work Cited

Feinberg, Leslie. "We Are All Works in Progress." *Reading and Writing on the Edge*. Eds. Deirdre Vinyard et al. Boston: Pearson, 2014. 99–106. Print. Mercury Reader Ser.

Different Values between America and China

SHUAI GU

Drawing on his experiences writing in different cultures, Gu enters into a dialogue with Fan Shen and Maxine Hong Kingston. Gu's well-developed personal examples explain and extend Shen's and Kingston's observations about writing across cultures.

Chinese ways of writing are really different from American English. Ever since I got into Englwrit 111, I was really confused about the structure of American writing. In China, everything is done indirectly and collectively, including our ways of expressing ourselves and through our writing. However, the American writing style emphasizes more on expressing individual thoughts and getting straight to the point of the topic. This is a tremendous difference with the Chinese writing styles. In this essay, I will compare and contrast the differences between standard American English and Chinese writing style based on indirectness and collectivism.

Chinese writing style likes to utilize poetic language to convey a message or idea indirectly. They avoid using blunt language to express their opinions and instead try to find a more mild way of implying. In China, if your writing style were too direct or abrupt, you would be considered as someone with low emotional intelligence. At the same time, this cultural value has an impact on my writing. In China, there is a kind of literary writing style called prose writing. I had used this type of writing style to write my essays in the past. This style of writing gives me a feeling of vagueness. When you read prose writing, it is hard to understand at first because the main idea is not directly implied within the first paragraph. It feels like as if you are walking in circles without a destination. In my perspective, this form of writing causes the proceeding paragraphs to create a certain background for the essay's conclusion. As author Fan Shen mentioned in his essay "The Classroom and the Wider Culture," "Roughly speaking, yijing is the process of creating a pictorial environment while reading a piece of literature" (147). "Yijing" or environmental portrayal is one of the most common methods used in prose writing. Shen also said that this "nonverbal, pictorial process leads directly to a higher ground of beauty and morality. Almost all critics in China agree that yijing is not a process of logical thinking—it is not a process of moving from the premises of an argument to its conclusion, which is the foundation of Western criticism" (147). I totally agree with Shen's opinion. It is because of yijing that Chinese writing tends to be illogical from the perspective of Standard American English. The goal of prose writing is to utilize the art of the environment to paint a vivid picture in the audience's minds.

In high school, my Chinese teacher assigned me to write an essay using the prose writing style. After the class, I had no idea about what I wanted to write. Hence, I just depicted the environment as much as possible. However, I still did not know what the main point of the essay was after I completed it. After my teacher read the essay, he told me that it was well written. I thought it was ridiculous since there was no logic in the essay. I did not have any ideas as to what I want to express before I initiated the essay. It was because I could not express my ideas directly and that there is no specific rule to estimate the essay. I can think about it, but I can never fully express it.

Collectivism is another form of writing in China. Due to historical reasons, China always refers back to Marxism and its collective form of writing, which forces people to link everything back to the view of collectivism. If anyone is too self-absorbed, they will be considered as egocentric. Thus, this awareness plays a crucial role in Chinese writing. In Chinese writing, "we" is more likely to be used than "I" in an essay. However, the word "I" is widely used in Standard American English (SAE). The SAE is more likely to respect the individual development and focus on individual thoughts. As Maxine Hong Kingston stated in her essay "Silence," "Was it out of politeness that this writer left off the strokes the way a Chinese has to write her own name small and crooked? No, it was not politeness; 'I' is a capital and 'you' is lowercase" (139). "I" is emphasized in Standard American English. As we all know, the capital word always represents "Noticing." Under no circumstance you can use "i" rather than "I," which shows the importance of the status of "I" in Standard American English.

I still remember that my writing professor taught me how to write an argument when I studied in China. She emphasized that if I have to demonstrate one point, I need to cite a large amount of examples from books or other sources rather than relying on my own experience, since personal experiences cannot represent common phenomena in the society. She assigned an assignment to write an essay about whether or not failure is the mother of success. In the essay, I cited a large amount of examples from actual sources. However, even though I myself obtained a lot of personal experiences about success and failure, I did not incorporate them into my essay because I had to follow the rules that my professor gave me.

Although the Standard American English writing is vastly different than Chinese writing, I still need to find ways to differentiate between the two. As an international student, learning Standard American English is a wonderful opportunity to gain access to a brand new style of writing. In fact, writing styles should be creative and informing, allowing us to express our own thoughts and beliefs while at the same time still flowing effectively. Therefore, the best way to offer more variety is by incorporating both the American and Chinese writing styles.

Works Cited

Kingston, Maxine Hong. "Silence." Vinyard et al. 137–141. Print.

Shen, Fan. "The Classroom and the Wider Culture: Identity as a Key to Learning English Composition." Vinyard et al. 142–151. Print.

Vinyard, Deirdre, et al., eds. *Reading and Writing on the Edge*. Boston: Pearson, 2014. Print. Mercury Reader Ser.

Assimilation: The Price to Pay

MERVEILLE I. KAZIMOTO

Kazimoto weaves together multiple sources to explore the complicated nature of assimilation and to ultimately argue for an America where "living bilingually, multi-culturally, and transnationally is acceptable." By incorporating an extended example throughout the essay, Kazimoto creates an argument that is both complex and cohesive.

For many years, immigration has been a subject of significant matter in this country. Given this history, it should not strike us as a surprise that the same subject still surfaces. Immigration remains a passionate topic across America, creating heated, controversial debates that oftentimes take the media by storm. America is traditionally referred to as a "melting pot," suggesting that all immigrants can be forged into Americans through the alchemy called assimilation. *Merriam-Webster Online* defines the verb "to assimilate" as "to adopt the ways of another culture" and "to fully become part of a different society, country, etc." Immigrants in America experience an ongoing pressure to conform to the culture and ways of their new home away from home. Immigrants undergo tension to quit their identities and allow themselves to be swollen by America. This tension is undeniably self-evident in my friend of Chinese background, Guotin, who chooses to nickname himself David as to make things simpler for his American friends and avoid all the "Sorry! What's your name again?" moments.

Every year, hundreds of thousands of immigrants flock to this country. Some legally, others undocumented. Some for study and job purposes, some to escape from different kinds of oppression. One thing we can all agree upon is that they all come to seek out the "American Dream." Perhaps it's time we dropped the old debate on whether immigrants are a burden or a blessing to America and start questioning how American society perceives them. My friend, Guotin, was born and raised in New York City in Chinatown to a family of Chinese immigrants. Decades ago, Guotin's parents were among the thousands of Chinese immigrants who flock to America. His family owns a restaurant, the typical Chinese family business. Guotin tells me that he goes to China every once and then to visit family and "connect with his origins." Contrary to what most people imagine, Guotin says the real China is nothing like Chinatown in New York. Guotin's world had been revolving around the American idea of what is Chinese because he is indeed American. All he knows about life and everything else he learnt from the American—well, the "so-not-American-not-so-really-Chinese"—Chinatown society in New York City.

However, that's not what people hear when he introduces himself. They hear: "I'm Asian," "I'm Chinese"! Americans subconsciously think one named "Guotin" can't be American because that name doesn't reflect American-ness as "Carl" and "David" or "Liam" and "Mason" do. The American people insist that immigrants have to assimilate and abide by the American ways in order to qualify as insiders. For that reason, Guotin is compelled to redesign his name to David. That way he is who he is, American. Yes, names are very monumental when it comes to what's American and what's not. As Michael Jones-Correa writes in his essay "How Immigrants are Marked as Outsiders,"

> [Immigrants] become insiders when their differences no longer affect the ways they interact with others, the opportunities they have for themselves and their families, and how they participate in politics.

> There is no clear dividing line between being an insider and an outsider. Individuals and groups whose families have spent many generations in the U.S. may feel some of both. However, three things set immigrants apart. ... The first of these is having a legally defined status and a pathway toward legal citizenship. ...

> The second is taking part in a shared language. ...

> The third is immigrants' perceptions of inclusion by the larger society.

Will naming themselves names that are less ethnic but rather "American"—or should I say European or Christian—help immigrants feel not excluded anymore? Maybe yes, maybe no! Who knows? It's such an intricate conundrum as one would put it!

Jones-Correa suggests that citizenship, social acceptance—whatever that means—and English fluency can upgrade immigrants' status from "outsiders" to "insiders." However, we know well that the acceptance of immigrants as insiders requires way more than just that. Many immigrants and their descendants have acquired citizenship, speak English very well, have jobs, and engage with their communities but are still referred to as the "other" or "outsider." For instance, when in 2013 American singer and actor Marc Anthony sang "God Bless America" at the 2013 MLB All-Star Game and 11-year-old Sebastien de la Cruz of *America's Got Talent* fame sang the national anthem at the NBA finals, both performances were received with racist criticism and protests from so-called patriotic Americans. The New York-born American-Puerto Rican megastar and Mexican-American prodigy were deemed as "un-American" and called "illegal aliens" (Reichard).

As the Declaration of Independence states, "We hold these truths to be self-evident, that all men are created equal, that they are endowed by their Creator with certain unalienable Rights, that among these are Life, Liberty and the Pursuit of Happiness." All men—not just white—are equal. Yet "Who are the real citizens of America?" remains one of the controversial themes in our debates. Two hundred years ago, an honest answer to these questions would have excluded not only slaves, women, and Asians but also Italians, Germans, Scotch-Irish, Catholics, and Jews. Immigrants love America and America loves immigrants (at least, this is what the founding fathers of America hoped for). There is no denying that the process of gaining inclusion and acceptance in American society is affected by the traditional American obsession with color and race. In her essay "Race Can Preclude Acceptance for Immigrants," Rose Cuison Villazor asserts that for many years discriminatory laws in America have made it difficult for immigrants of color to cross the "threshold of belonging" through denial of citizenship or unequal citizenship. She concludes that, "The explanation for why some immigrant groups are considered Americans while some continue to be deemed outsiders must include the links between whiteness, citizenship and what it means to be an American."

For decades, immigrants have proven their loyalty and dedication towards this country by working hard, paying taxes, and contributing in the well-being of their communities. They have devoted themselves to chasing the American dream. Immigrants are not just "immigrants": they are our cooks, they teach our kids, and they are our neighbors. They certainly are one of us. What pains many immigrants is that America shows less, if any, appreciation towards them and chooses to consider them as a burden, as that one extra luggage you wish you did not bring with you. Contrary to the popular belief that immigrants are freeloaders who come to this country to exhaust social services, immigrants do contribute to this country through paying taxes and Social Security. That's right, immigrants pay taxes. Immigrants shouldn't need to "assimilate" or conform to the idea of who is the true American to be perceived as fellow insiders. As Richard Rodriguez puts it in his essay "The North American," "ASSIMILATION HAPPENS. One doesn't get up in the morning, as an immigrant child in America, and think to oneself, 'How much of an American will I become today?' … Culture is fluid" (Rodriguez 74). One can imagine an America where living bilingually, multi-culturally, and transnationally is acceptable and not anything "alien." A society that accepts the name "Guotin" as its own.

Works Cited

"Assimilate." *Merriam-Webster Online*. Merriam-Webster, n.d. Web. 26 Feb. 2016.

Jones-Correa, Michael. "How Immigrants Are Marked as Outsiders." *New York Times*. New York Times, 18 Nov. 2012. Web. 19 Mar. 2015.

Reichard, Raquel. "9 Things Latinos are Tired of Explaining to Everyone Else." *Mic*. Mic Network Inc., 4 Mar. 2015. Web. 18 Mar. 2015.

Rodriguez, Richard. "The North American." *Reading and Writing on the Edge*. Eds. Deirdre Vinyard et al. Boston: Pearson, 2014. 99–106. Print. Mercury Reader Ser.

Villazor, Rose Cuison. "Race Can Preclude Acceptance for Immigrants." *New York Times*. New York Times, 5 June 2013. Web. 20 Mar. 2015.

Identities throughout Generations

SARA MACDONALD

Through the use of vivid details, MacDonald sets up a thoughtful reflection on immigration, identity, and generational difference. She brings in Bharati Mukherjee's "Two Ways to Belong in America" to deepen and extend her analysis of her family's experiences with immigration and identity.

My grandmother resides in a rehabilitation center that smells overwhelmingly of cleaning chemicals and day old pot roast. I call her in the mornings and visit her on the weekends that I am home from school. She looks eerie surrounded by white. White walls, white sheets, even her face has lost the color it once held so intensely. I sit at the end of her bed, and she asks me the same question that I hear every time I see her, without exception:

"Do you remember picking strawberries in the backyard with Mez Mama? Oh, she loved you girls."

Mez Mama, the Armenian saying for grandmother, is what my entire family refers to my great grandmother as. I have built up what I'm sure is an imaginary memory of this in my mind from being told the story so often. I envision my sister and I holding Mez Mama's hand, tracing the strawberry bushes that no longer stand in the yard, as she speaks in her native language to us. I hold onto other memories from my childhood in Watertown, the town where a majority of my Armenian family lives. Walking through it all looks something like this:

I am holding a plastic bag under a ladder as my mother drops down grape leaves from my grandmother's cherished grapevine. The leaves, wrapped around a hand-built wooden post, are a jungle in the sky through my small eyes. I am sitting in a kitchen chair that is much too big and covered in too much uncomfortable plastic, trying to roll lamb into these same leaves for one of many traditional Armenian meals. I am laying with photographs spilling onto the floor around me as I look into my family's past life. I am pouting with my sister in the basement of my cousin's house as our relatives speak in a language that we cannot understand. I am curled into my great aunt's lap and she is kissing both of my cheeks, pinching both of my cheeks. She does this over and over, telling me that I am her "cherub." Years later, I find out this means fat little angel.

I feel disconnected from my culture because my mother tried so hard to make sure that she was not defined by it. I think back one year to my mother leaning against the frame of my bedroom door, apologizing to me for the way that she speaks ill of my grandfather. She tells me that her father was always of good faith and good intentions, but he had heavy opinions and strong restrictions. She tells me of the somewhat secluded life she led growing up, how she never felt normal. No sleepovers, clothes that never matched her classmates', and God forbid she date without approval. She often tells my sister and me about her struggling to get permission to go to college, to escape some of the expectations that came along with being so tightly wound into the Armenian culture. Though my mother loves her father infinitely, I think that she associates a lot of her cultural values with him and his overbearing ways. She and her siblings were of the first in their generation to marry outside of the ethnicity. Growing up, it never occurred to me that I was something more than simply American. I knew that my mother's side was different from my father's. I knew that my mother could speak this sort of mystic other language. I knew that sometimes, on holidays especially, I ate food that held a more powerful flavor than what we normally had.

To my family, Mez Mama was magic. I hear about her always. I see my mother go back in time whenever she recalls growing up with her. I think what my family admires the most about her is the way that she continued to gracefully embody all of their Armenian traditions when she came over to America. How she connected them all to a place they could have so easily forgotten and left behind. Just as Mez Mama did, my grandmother clung to her Armenian identity. This is evident in her surroundings and her every mannerism. It is something I pick up on whenever I go for my routine visits. Sometimes her house feels like an entirely different planet than my home. There is a line that starts at my head and ends at my toes, drawn straight down the middle of me, separating my Armenian heritage from my American one.

Similar to my family, Bharati Mukherjee addresses carrying on and living with her native identity and traditions in America in her essay "Two Ways to Belong in America." Mukherjee and her sister, Mira, were born and raised in India and moved to America, where they found themselves going down different paths. Mira got married to an Indian student and still dreams of her home in India. Mukherjee married an American despite her family's customs (45).

Feeling betrayed by the laws targeting legal immigrants, Mira threatens to pick up and go back to India. Mukherjee understands her sister's fears and concerns, but feels less strongly about them. When addressing the issue, Mukherjee writes, "America spoke to me—I married it—I embraced the demotion from expatriate aristocrat to immigrant nobody, surrendering those thousands of years of 'pure culture,' the saris, the delightfully accented English. [Mira] retained them all" (47). Just as my Armenian family came to America and split into different cultural directions down the line of generations, Mukherjee and her sister each created new ways to live with their Indian traditions. Though both of the girls feel connected to their lives in India, their time in America brought a new meaning to each of their identities. Mez Mama and my grandfather, like Mira, stood strong on the grounds of their cultural identity. Skip down a few generations, and my mother leans more towards Mukherjee's mindset. I find myself somewhere in between, without as much of a choice as Mira, Mukherjee, and my relatives had.

Today, I carry around bits of both sides of my family. My mother tells me more and more stories of my grandfather. I make promises to come cook with my grandmother when she returns home from rehab. My mother gives me turquoise rings on special occasions, and we exchange "evil eye" trinkets whenever we come across them. When I am nervous or troubled, I touch them knowing that to most Armenians, they are emblems of good luck and protection.

We choose to belong, or to not belong, to our cultures. We have the ability to cut ties just the same as we do to build new ones and maintain old ones. There is, however, no avoiding our own history. We are a combination of our family's past and our own present and future. Mez Mama decided to hold onto as much as she could of her culture when coming to America, with my grandfather following close in her footsteps. My mother chose to let go of the parts of her Armenian culture that she felt suffocated by and to pick up parts of the American culture that she felt could be a better part of her. Mira felt she would be "happier to live in America as expatriate Indian than as an immigrant American" (48). Mukherjee found herself ready to settle into the American culture while putting less stress on her Indian identity. There is no right or wrong way to adapt to a new home. When immigrants come to a different country, there is no ultimatum of picking one identity over another. I cannot claim to know much about leaving one's culture behind and picking up a new one, but I believe that we are a blend of the cultures that we choose to surround and define ourselves by. Who is to say where the Mukherjee sisters' children may end up, what they will hand down to their children, and their children, and on, and on? Who is to say how much of my Armenian culture will disappear and reappear throughout the generations of my family? We live with and pass on the identities that we choose to, no matter what country we find ourselves in.

Work Cited

Mukherjee, Bharati. "Two Ways to Belong in America." *Reading and Writing on the Edge*. Eds. Deirdre Vinyard et al. Boston: Pearson, 2014. 44–48. Print. Mercury Reader Ser.

Shy

JESSICA MAZZOLA

Mazzola explains how shyness functions as a border in her life by describing her experiences in a specific context: the classroom. By analyzing her personal experience, Mazzola illustrates how borders can protect and define as well as separate and isolate.

I was trying to talk to my teacher. There were too many background voices and noises, so I risked speaking louder than I usually do for her to hear me. Just my luck, everyone paused in speech the minute I started. When I felt the room look at me, I silenced myself and shrank in my seat from embarrassment, waiting for the moment to pass. It feels like my heart literally shrinks in size every time this happens; I can no longer speak and all I want to do is disappear.

This and many similar experiences like it have plagued me for as long as I can remember. I'm not sure why I'm so shy, but to me it feels like an invisible border, blocking me from many different opportunities I could've obtained. Whenever I experience it, I feel trapped in. I can't make myself be heard or seen. It's like a fail-safe boundary I've built for myself so that I won't get made fun of or get embarrassed by whatever I could say. I feel kind of negatively towards this. I believe certain things require more confidence and independence in order to achieve more success. However, I also don't feel that badly towards it because it's how I avoid being noticed by people who could hurt me in response to any confidence I reveal.

I used to sit farther away from the front of the room, and this introduced a conflict. What if I needed to ask a question? I didn't want to go right out and ask for fear of it sounding silly in addition to everyone noticing me. In the past, I'd felt victimized and embarrassed from this kind of situation; I knew how it played out. I'd raise my solitary hand to ask a question, and when I'd get picked I'd ask my question, only to be asked to speak louder. I'd start to feel warm when I spoke loud enough for all to hear, and it would become worse when I realized I had just missed what the teacher already said. Conclusively, I would be both noticed and singled out as not very bright. My face would flush red and once again I'd shrink in my seat waiting for invisibility to cloak me from the prying stares of my classmates. This instance is also representative of my boundary because I can't ask the questions I need to understand important concepts. I always try to figure out a path around this obstacle, but the truth is I'd probably be way better off by being direct.

To me these experiences are sound representations of my border. I chose classroom experiences because they are where I have encountered my border the most. They are also where the encounters have been the most memorable. When you have been with a group of people since elementary school, and everyone has made their friends, it's difficult to show much of yourself without being judged. Some people are relatively nice but they won't look to you for a friend, so you do not do the same in return. I did not have a lot of friends in school, but I was okay with that because the ones I had were all very close. However, because of this, I had all these situations where I was surrounded by people I did not know well. Thus, I had no motivation to be outgoing or to express myself, and of course I wasn't going to even if there was motivation.

These experiences I've had are especially significant because my shyness is one of the sole parts of me that I fully understand. I understand how it works into my everyday behavior and how that behavior comes back to affect me. A little shyness every once in a while in certain situations is okay, but having it pop up all the time in social situations or in a classroom is not okay. In a classroom, I won't be able to understand the material as well if I don't suck it up and ask questions. In a social situation, I won't be very skilled at making good friends and interacting with them. This is my border, and every time I come across a situation where I am singled out, I feel it stop me from expressing myself as a way of protection, as a block.

I feel that shyness can be considered a border because even if it is mostly assumed to be fixable, it's always been a part of me. In my eyes, it's never going to go away. Shyness is always going to be present when I'm in a social situation. It prevents me from going that extra length to be outgoing, to interact, and to ask questions. In truth, I feel that I can lessen this quality and make it less prominent so that I won't be as in the dark. I won't have as big of an obstacle blocking me from the successes I could gain in my life. However, overall I do not feel that I can completely just make it disappear. In my eyes, I can't completely cross this border.

Running in the Same Place

OSHIOMAH OYAGESHIO

After using personal experience to capture the reader's attention, Oyageshio incorporates multiple sources to construct an argument about racism that considers local, national, and digital contexts. Oyageshio resists a tidy conclusion to his essay, instead asking readers to consider the larger, complex questions he raises. Please note that this essay includes an image of graffiti containing a word that Merriam-Webster Online *describes as "perhaps the most offensive and inflammatory racial slur in English."*

A couple of weeks ago, I spent my spring break on the UMass campus. I was on the bus back from the town center, and I got off at the stop closest to the dining commons. I walked to Hampshire Dining Commons. As I entered the building, I was overwhelmed by the number of people here compared to the relatively empty rest of campus, probably because it was the only DC open. I found a seat and I went on to fill my plate with food. Pizza, pasta, dessert—I was hungry. As I sat down, I checked my phone to browse the Yik Yak app. Yik Yak is a social media app where anyone can freely post their thoughts, called "yaks," anonymously, and the viewers can comment, up vote, or down vote on the posted yak. The yaks are often locked to particular locations, such as college campuses. It is used by students as a means of discussion, information, and as an outlet for venting; it's like an anonymous bulletin board.

As I scrolled down through the yaks, one caught my attention. It read, "The black boy in the blue backpack is a thug and should leave Amherst." Let's call this anonymous Yakker, X. To paint a clearer picture...

I am black.

I was wearing a blue backpack.

All sorts of emotions started to flood: anger, confusion, sadness, denial. I clicked on the comments of the yak. Someone asked why he said that. X went on to say, "Someone bumped into him in the bus and he threatened a boy on the bus with a knife." I began to think back to my time on the bus. Did I really do this? Was I possessed by some spirit that made me violently threaten people? Last I checked I'm a pacifist, and I don't usually have the confidence to talk to strangers on the bus, let alone threaten them.

In my denial phase I started to mentally fish for reasons why I wasn't the one in the yak. I recalled my journey from the bus to the dining commons. I was certain there were no other black boys with blue backpacks who rode a bus like me. I started to realize what this situation really was. It was a racially charged statement... *against me*. Why? I rode the bus seated alone, plugged into my headphones. Apparently I'm a thug for doing that. X went out of his or her way to fabricate a false story about me. I looked at my food, and I lost my appetite. My stomach was already filled with knots. I looked around the dining commons. Could X be here? I didn't know. I wasn't comfortable. Paranoia consumed my thoughts. X was lurking behind the shadows, protected by the anonymity of the Internet. X could be someone I see every day, someone I smile at, someone living on my floor. There's no way to know. I checked Yik Yak again so I could take a screenshot of the yak, but it had more than five down votes, so it was deleted. For a moment I was happy that other people felt that his yak was racist but X had already done the damage. I had every right to feel safe and confident eating in the dining commons, but X managed to rip that away from me that afternoon.

What I experienced is called "ethno-stress," as described by Josh Odam, a fellow black UMass student. He describes ethno-stress, in a *Collegian* essay, as "mental and social pressures students of color face while in predominantly white spaces." He writes about this because he has experienced his own version of ethno-stress. Last year, he travelled to Ferguson, Missouri, for a rally following the Michael Brown shooting. Upon his arrival back to his dorm on campus, he saw this graffiti on his door:

Courtesy of Josh Odam/Daily Collegian

He writes about this ordeal in "#WrongDoor: Ethno-stress and Racially Charged Attacks on the UMass Campus." Odam gives an example of ethno-stress as being a minority in a large lecture hall that is primarily white but to add to that having "social and mental pressures" of racist situations like his and mine. He writes that it's these kind of situations where ethno-stress "rears its ugly head." One of the commenters on the article, who goes by "Ed Cutting," makes some interesting points. He writes that the graffiti must have been made in a short time period before Odam arrived because the Residential Assistants wouldn't have allowed that to stay up for so long, deducing that the writer of this may have even known Odam. The miscreant may have known that he was a secretary of diversity for the Student Government Association. Did Odam's credentials make the writer of this uncomfortable, arouse anger, hatred or threat? Probably.

The university held a Town Hall Meeting because of this incident and two other racist vandalism acts that occurred in the student dorms. There were a couple of *Collegian* articles that covered this meeting. In the article, "Racist Vandalism Prompts Emergency Meeting to Discuss Race Relations and Diversity," Catherine Ferris, a *Collegian* reporter, quotes the president of the Muslim Students Association, Elkhansaa Elguenaoui, who spoke in the meeting, as saying, "I think it's time to talk about such a topic. A topic that's so manifested in where we live. We live under an illusion that it's in the past, but it's 2014, and it's still huge. We've pushed it under the rug. It's time to dig it up and deal with it." This comment takes me back to my Yik Yak experience. I remember soon after that experience talking to my friend about this in my dorm. He explained, "[X] is a coward and probably a fat troll. Normal socially acceptable people don't do that. It doesn't matter—just forget about it, man. You're 6'3 and muscular—you can probably take him down." Although I appreciated his sentiment, I got into a heated debate with him. I argued that people that appear to be "normal" can be racist, and I can't just "forget about it." Like Elguenaoui said at the meeting, we need to deal with this. We need to expose what is going on in the shadows and not pretend everything's okay.

I worry that racism and its ignorance will forever exist. I feel it's easier for whites to say things like "Just forget about it," "It's 2015; racism isn't really a thing anymore," or "There's no need to protest in Massachusetts; it's a liberal state." They haven't been in our shoes or faced the prejudice blacks have faced, but they still tell us how we should feel about it. Just to be clear I am not saying all whites think this way. The most offensive statement I've heard regarding this issue was during a discussion in the dorm. My friend (the same one I narrated my Yik Yak incident to) told me that the whole "Black Lives Matter" movement should be altered to "All Lives Matter." We had a verbal argument that spanned three days because of this. In fact we still argue till now. Not only on his opinion on Black Lives Matter but other things like how the society should be more grateful to police officers for the good they do and stop painting cops with a racist brush. I argue that we know the police are good. Nonetheless, it is their job to exhibit fair justice, especially when making arrests, regardless if they think suspects are guilty. It is not a requirement to applaud the police for doing the right thing. Although we can, we don't have to. It is their job.

There has been another instance of ethno-stress I've experienced. There is another social media app called FADE that is similar to Yik Yak. Each post is called a "Fade," and in this app there is a section dedicated for Fades from UMass and Westfield State University (WSU). There was a post, by someone who I will call "L," that read, "Stop the #blacklivesmatter shit. All lives matter. Just stop doing stupid shit and comply with the law." What was even more astounding was that it had 153 up votes. One hundred and fifty three people (and counting) in UMass and WSU agreed that blacks should stop doing "stupid shit" and comply with the law. Don't other races do "stupid shit" as well, or is it that black peoples'"shit" is worse than others? Another question to these people is this: Do you think that us blacks are supremacists and think only our lives matter? Of course we don't, but blacks are the ones that are unjustly gunned down by white police officers. Take the Eric Garner and Michael Brown cases for instance. Whether the victims were criminals or not, they deserved fair treatment especially when they are arrested. We say "Black Lives Matter" because we are hypervigilant and afraid. That slogan is a defense mechanism, and we are condemned by people like L for having such a slogan. Fortunately, it is possible to have chats on FADE, so I instigated a conversation with this person. After I presented these points to L, this was his reply:

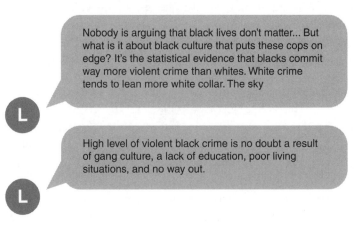

> Nobody is arguing that black lives don't matter... But what is it about black culture that puts these cops on edge? It's the statistical evidence that blacks commit way more violent crime than whites. White crime tends to lean more white collar. The sky

L

> High level of violent black crime is no doubt a result of gang culture, a lack of education, poor living situations, and no way out.

L

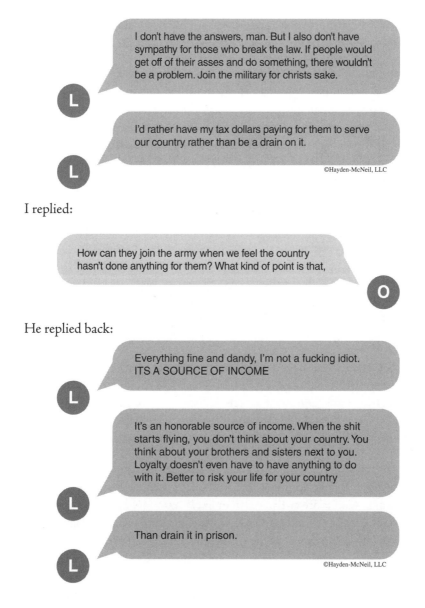

I replied:

He replied back:

I'm not really sure what L means by black culture putting cops "on edge." According to an online report "Homicide Trends in the United States, 1980–2008" by the US Department of Justice, blacks accounted for 52.5% of homicide offenders from 1980 to 2008 while whites accounted for 45.3% (Cooper and Smith 3). So is it the 7% disparity in homicide rates that makes cops hypervigilant? L and others like him believe that cops see a black teenager on a street and assume he might be a criminal because of this supposed "black culture." Why can't cops look at Barack Obama or Ben Carson and think that kid on the street may be our future president or the next great brain surgeon?

In my opinion, the "All Lives Matter" argument is very weak. It's just like saying that we should have "masculinists" in addition to feminists, and colleges shouldn't have women's studies departments but only gender studies departments. Just because all genders matter should we also discount the fact that women also have had a history of oppression? If the pro "All Lives Matter" believers think we should start saying "All Genders Matter," we have a greater problem on our hands.

I feel one of the main reasons for this everlasting argument on race occurs because different people have different predisposed mindsets. Are these mindsets because of the color of our skin? Maybe. After I narrated my Yik Yak incident to some of my white friends I got some interesting responses. There was the friend I described earlier, but another one said, "It could have been a joke"; he later on rebuffed his statement after giving it more thought. Why the initial statement, though? Does he believe that we live in a perfect world without racism where X's statement could have been a joke?

Do black people have a shrouded judgement that makes us look like victims in racial situations? Do white people have a predisposed mindset that blacks take racial situations too seriously and feel we always overreact? Does that make everyone prejudiced? Possibly. Maybe racism isn't just black or white (no pun intended). It's like a spectrum and most people fit somewhere along the line.

Over the years there have been great milestones in combating racism in America. I still feel we are somewhat in the same position as we were a century ago only with more civilized dynamics. It has moved from black people being chained and forced to work in farms to cyber hate crimes and ignorance. Obviously those situations are very different but the latter could be viewed as an evolved, less barbaric version of the former. We've gone from physical oppression to socio-economic and psychological subjugation (e.g., ethnostress). In physics, the law of conservation of matter states that energy can neither be created nor destroyed but is converted from one form to another. Maybe the same can be said for racism. Is it going to be in a perpetual state of evolution, or will it end?

Racism is not dead.

Will it ever be?

Works Cited

Cutting, Ed. Weblog comment. "#WrongDoor: Ethno-stress and Racially Charged Attacks on the UMass Campus." *Massachusetts Daily Collegian.* The Massachusetts Daily Collegian, 16 Oct. 2014. Web. 23 Apr. 2015.

Cooper, Alexia, and Erica L. Smith. "Homicide Trends in the United States, 1980–2008." U.S. Bureau of Justice Statistics. *Bureau of Justice Statistics.* U.S. Department of Justice Office of Justice Programs, 16 Nov. 2011. Web. 26 Feb. 2016.

Ferris, Catherine. "Racist Vandalism Prompts Emergency Meeting to Discuss Race Relations and Diversity." *Massachusetts Daily Collegian.* The Massachusetts Daily Collegian, 16 Oct. 2014. Web. 23 Apr. 2015.

Odam, Josh. "#WrongDoor: Ethno-stress and Racially Charged Attacks on the UMass Campus." *Massachusetts Daily Collegian.* The Massachusetts Daily Collegian, 16 Oct. 2014. Web. 23 Apr. 2015.

Just Another Language

JOSÉ E. REYES

Reyes crafts an argument for changing second language instruction, incorporating personal experience with essays by Amy Tan and Maxine Hong Kingston. In addition to describing the process of language acquisition, Reyes sheds light into the emotional and social dimensions of learning a new language.

It takes approximately three months to learn the basics of a new language. People who are learning Standard American English as a second language face a large number of obstacles. One of these obstacles is evident in Amy Tan's "Mother Tongue," which focuses on the struggles of her mother as an immigrant in America. From personal experiences I know that another obstacle people who are learning Standard American English as a second language in America face is that you are thought of as different and looked down upon. This feeling is shared in Maxine Hong Kingston's "Silence" where she describes the way she felt when she had to speak English in front of other people who spoke proficient Standard American English. People who are learning Standard American English (SAE) as a second language are not given a fair chance and are looked down upon, which affects their self-esteem in a negative way. They are alienated and thought of as different by those who already speak SAE. A way to fix this would be to teach it in a different way, changing the way in which the class is perceived.

Immigrants who speak English as a second language and do not speak perfect SAE are not given a fair chance at many things. Tan's mother is a good example of this happening. Tan explains to the reader how when her mother went to department stores, banks, and restaurants they would "not take her seriously, did not give her good service, pretended not to understand her, or even acted as if they did not hear her" (133). This happened to Tan's mother just because she was speaking with an accent, or speaking "broken" English (132). These people who knew how to speak SAE were purposely alienating Tan's mother simply because of the way she spoke. It got to the point where "when I [Tan] was fifteen, she used to have me call people on the phone to pretend I was she" (133). That way, the same people who were alienating Tan's mother and treating her differently because she was not able to speak SAE the way they were able to would stop treating her differently. The only way Tan's mother was going to be treated equally was if her daughter, who did not speak with an accent, spoke for her. This is a big obstacle which immigrants who do not speak SAE as well as others face almost every day, whereas someone who did speak SAE well would not have to go through this.

The way which Standard American English is taught to students who are learning English as a second language can be degrading and feels like people are looking down upon you. I am someone who learned English as a second language while knowing how to fluently speak Spanish. The third grade is one of the most important years in school. That is where the foundation to properly learn the language is set. Everything builds upon the foundation built in the third grade. I spend my third grade year in the Dominican Republic. I moved to America in the fifth grade and was put in an English Second Language class (ESL). The curriculum of this class consisted of the regular third grade English book. At first I was not bothered with starting to learn English this way. But then when the sixth grade came around and we were still using the same third grade book, I was furious; it was not enough of a challenge. After learning from the same book for one entire school year, I wanted to push myself. I asked the teacher if she was able to teach me from the sixth grade book, and she agreed. I am sure my teacher was not underestimating how smart I was. However, the people who were making the curriculum for the ESL classes were. They did not believe that a sixth grader who is only on his second year of learning English could handle anything above of what a normal third grader could handle. I felt like I was being looked down upon, as if I was not smart enough. It is degrading to think that a sixth grader can only handle the workload of a third grader for two straight years, only because they are learning English as second language.

Another obstacle immigrants who cannot speak proper SAE face is being alienated because of the way they speak. Going through middle school as an immigrant who is still in the process of learning English was not easy. I was constantly picked on because of the way I spoke. One time, in my seventh grade English class, it was my turn to read. The paragraph had words which I wasn't able to pronounce properly. As if they were part of a choir, the whole class burst into laughter when I read the word "character" with the *ch* sounding like the word "chair." Feeling like I was being looked down upon by those in power and having people make fun of the way I spoke affected my self-esteem in a negative way. Kingston also felt this way when she was learning English. In her essay Kingston described how she was embarrassed to speak SAE in front of others because "the same voice came out ... bones rubbing jagged against one another" (141). Kingston knew that when she spoke the rest of the kids were going to make fun of her because she was different. It was bringing her self-esteem way down and making her not want to speak. But of course, people like us would have to fight through the obstacles and speak our way out of it. Even if those who spoke SAE the "right way" were still alienating us and making fun of us.

The way that Standard American English is taught to immigrants who are learning it as a second language needs to change. This current way of going from easy to hard in one step is not working. The basics should be taught in an easy to understand way, but the class should get progressively harder. Right now people who are learning English as a second language are being treated as if they were not smart enough to handle hard coursework. English is being treated as if it is some sort of impossible language and the people teaching it cannot challenge those who are learning it. Also, the way it is being perceived needs to change. It would be a lot more comforting if instead of always referring to the class as an "English second language class" to just learning another language. If those who are teaching change the perception of the class, then the rest of the people will follow. I was once guilty of thinking about English as my second language, but now I use it more than Spanish.

Works Cited

Kingston, Maxine Hong. "Silence." Vinyard et al. 137–141. Print.

Tan, Amy. "Mother Tongue." Vinyard et al. 131–136. Print.

Vinyard, Deirdre, et al., eds. *Reading and Writing on the Edge*. Boston: Pearson, 2014. Print. Mercury Reader Ser.

The Challenges of Assimilating

WEI WEI

Wei brings in essays by Richard Rodriguez and Bharati Mukherjee as she establishes her own stance on assimilation and acculturation. By putting her own experiences into dialogue with Rodriguez's and Mukherjee's, Wei reveals the complexity of assimilating to a different culture.

For me, the term "assimilation" is difficult to define. It is a complex and reactionary relationship between two entities that adapt to new changes in certain environments, like an immigrant in a foreign country for example. In this case, there are two primary possible outcomes for this interaction: one entity is influenced by the other *or* neither is affected. A person immersed into a new culture and introduced to new customs or ideas is likely to be affected socially, culturally, or even emotionally by this new environment. I am a student who is studying abroad, so I am confronted with assimilation all the time. Some people find it easy, comfortable, and enriching to adapt, while others might feel assimilation is not necessary or conducive to one's own individual development. As for me, while I feel it is important to maintain my strong ties to traditional Chinese culture, I am also open to absorbing new information at the same time. It takes patience, effort, and understanding to familiarize myself with a new culture and new customs. Actually, I'm hesitant to embrace certain aspects of American culture simply because it can be intimidating and perhaps I just lack the courage and time. Even though I plan on staying in America for only four years, I can't help but question how much I really need to assimilate to American culture, how much I want to assimilate to American culture, or if it's in my best interest to just do what I know and feel comfortable with from my own culture and keep close to Chinese friends. Until now, I really didn't know the answer.

When I think about what it is to be American or the distinctiveness of American culture I immediately associate them with behavior and self-expression. This is more clearly outlined by American "author" (critic? scholar?—I don't know) Richard Rodriguez, who wrote that young people are "already moving into a world in which skin or tattoo or ornament or movement or commune or sexuality or drug are the organizing principles of their identity" (74). These attributes certainly play a role in character development, but not one that I feel is distinctly "American" necessarily. I don't believe American culture can be accurately characterized only in this way. There is much more I've realized.

As a foreigner in the midst of day-to-day collisions with American culture, I've come to realize that it is not these principles that Rodriguez mentions on their own that is important, but rather, how these principles manifest themselves into social markers of independence. But the meaning of American culture to someone born and raised in America and to a foreigner who only knows what the media allows calls for very different perspectives. I believe Rodriguez just encounters a few sides of American culture; there's more about it, such as the pop music, rap, freedom, and adventure… In addition, it is hard to say a person who has a tattoo and is white must be American, and we cannot say a person who is wearing a suit is not an American. When I was walking on the street, there were so many people with tattoos, which is another thing I really want to try but cannot. I believe Americans would regard tattoos as a way which can show their beauty and personalities, but in China and even in most parts of Asia, it is a bad thing to have a tattoo. Because when those manager seeing the tattoo, people would fail in the job interviews, so I need to avoid having one. Another feature of American culture is dressing. American girls like to wear leggings and trend to sports style, and men trend to wear casual clothes instead of dress shirts. Actually, I bought leggings before, but I never wore them. I think this is not me, and I feel really strange with leggings. The reason maybe is I am a Chinese inside of my body.

Saying about learning assimilation, behavior must be the most profound thing because it needs to accumulate from how you look and what you experience, which means it has no short cut. To cross the national border to reach assimilation requires a lot of time and exercises. An outsider will never know how to associate in a school party, like I had not heard the word "homecoming party" before I attended school in America. A person who acts like a local would be easier to be considered a pure American.

Sometimes, even if you have the thought of embracing a new culture, you do not have the chance. I was living in China for most of my life, which means I have already known most of Chinese customs and culture. One person who had completed the assimilation of being an American is named Bharati Mukherjee. She also has the feeling about involving into a new culture: "I embraced the demotion from expatriate aristocrat to immigrant nobody, surrounding those thousands of years of 'pure culture,' the saris, the delightfully accented English" (47). I found the term "pure culture" is really attracting for me—does the term mean the culture of the original country? Or just mean those years that she spent in her motherland? However, I agree with both of the explanations. Although some people would like to vote the opposite view, they think those saris, the delightful accent are not a problem. But I would say even the delightfully accented English can bring a lot of troubles. I remember in one of the discussion classes, the TA is a Chinese, and when she talked with a delightful accent, there are two students laughed at her. I believe those students are not respected the TA; although she has the ability to teach the course, she just be laughed at because of the accent. So it seems like changing the accent and changing the behavior are very difficult but important things. On the one hand, I think the start to becoming a real citizen of another country is to embrace the whole culture, which needs to happen in some conditions. The writer is an immigrant; she has the right to stay in this continent and find a good job. She can live a wonderful life if she tries really hard to change her accent and dressing style, but this is just for those people who had the chance to stay for decades. On the contrary, some people do not have the opportunities to stay for a long period in another country, such as students who are studying abroad or those workers who are sent to a foreign country for one or two years.

For those people like me, I believe it is better to stay outside of the culture, not entirely, but acting in a comfortable way. If you want to involve into a new culture but are not able to, you need to know the truth that learning a new culture is the hardest thing because it takes two years to learn a language when you are little, and maybe using more than one decade to learn the behavior of a culture. Even with the greatest effort, you still need a long time to absorb the new information. Actually, being an outsider is a good thing for me because an outsider can feel the differences between two countries clearly, and I can find out the advantages and disadvantages independently. In this way, people can learn good things from different parts of other cultures and continually decide which things to ignore, adopt, or replace in their own lives. But there are some drawbacks: an outsider is easier to exclude, so it becomes difficult to break through certain social barriers, get involved with certain events or happenings, and thus harder to make local friends. Being an insider, people need to change their own habits, give up their own customs. But in this way, they can get more freedom and have less pressure living in the new country.

It seems hard to complete the assimilation to a culture, but I believe the best way we can do is following our heart, learning the good things from the new culture, and then substitute the outdated part of the old culture. By doing this, we can improve ourselves and make the trip worthy.

Works Cited

Mukherjee, Bharati. "Two Ways to Belong in America." Vinyard et al. 44–48. Print.

Rodriguez, Richard. "The North American." Vinyard et al. 66–76. Print.

Vinyard, Deirdre, et al., eds. *Reading and Writing on the Edge*. Boston: Pearson, 2014. Print. Mercury Reader Ser.

The Challenges of Assimilating

Part 2

Writing from and
across Contexts:
Essays from
College Writing

Inquiring into Self

Preface

College Writing begins by asking students to examine the "self," or one of our many selves, as a text in a unit called "Inquiring into Self." The self, after all, is a text that absolutely must be read and re-read with great attentiveness, for it shapes how we understand, interpret, and interact with the world. Using the writing process (generative writing and reading, composing and revising, giving and receiving feedback to and from fellow writers, and editing), students are asked to discover new insights about how their contexts have shaped them. The challenge is to read their stories and bodies as histories and to begin to re-see themselves through the lenses of social contexts—e.g., towns, churches, athletic teams, ethnic communities, and more. Here, students write meaningfully about their own lives. The following essays illustrate this inquiry into self and invite a close audience of classmates to engage with each writer's experiences and critical reflections.

Finding the Music

LIAM DILLON

Liam Dillon shifts tone and voice in his essay to echo his movement from description to reflection and analysis. Initially he uses a colloquial voice peppered with biting wit to characterize the atmosphere of a local music venue. He contrasts the patrons of the early show, middle-aged people who come to drink in the nostalgia of 1980s "dad rock," with the UMass crowd that arrives for the late show. Ultimately, his tone becomes serious as his observations lead him to understand what attracts these dual audiences—the power of live music to recreate our pasts, lose ourselves in the present, and inspire our dreams for the future.

The Iron Horse Music Hall, a sit-down venue that usually caters to a demographic at least 30 years older than I am, brings in musical acts that can be described with no better term than "dad rock." These bands were cool in the 80s. They were on MTV back when there was music on MTV, though you really had to be there when it was happening to have heard of them. That, or maybe you have spent some time with your dad's record collection, as I have. Now these bands have been reduced to playing nostalgia shows in small, dark venues for middle-class married couples who want to sit down and order a ten dollar, not-quite-pint-sized glass of Guinness and some slightly-better-than-cheap, but similarly overpriced white wine. They want to be on their way home by ten because they went to work that day, and even though tomorrow is Saturday, they still can't stay out as late as they could ten years ago.

Tonight the Iron Horse looks different. It's ten-thirty—time for the second show of the night. The middle-aged, middle-class work force has gone home, and the tables that were front and center have been cleared out to make a pit in front of the stage. As I take a seat at a table off to the side of the stage, I take in my surroundings. The room is filled with college kids: bearded guys in flannels outnumbered by girls I can tell are from the university, not one of the surrounding liberal arts colleges because of the length of their hair and the location of their nose piercings. They all sway, to varying degrees, to the opening band, a local band, and their enjoyably distinct jangly indie/surf/ dance rock amalgamation.

All of this resonates with me. There is something deeply satisfying about seeing people my own age not simply at a show, but reveling in live music. This is how countless movies, songs, and stories have been depicted to me about every decade from the 60s to the 90s. And the band? Just a group of guys who go to the same school as I do, just a few years older, making their own music. Music that is not only good, but that people come out to shows for and know the lyrics to. This is something that has been missing from my life: an entire social phenomenon based on the production and delivery of art, another chance for one to distinguish oneself from the crowd that doesn't involve being on the football team or being especially good looking or socially apt. It was non-existent at my small, preppy high school where my shaggy hair caused confusion because it wasn't associated with lacrosse or hockey. Where anything artistic or musical that you couldn't put on your college resume was completely foreign. Where all anyone seemed to care about was what prestigious private education you were moving on to, or just what your parents could afford. Now in college, in the part of campus I'm living, everything seems to be a continuation of high school. For whatever reason, all these people have ended up at a public university, but they still seem to be doing the same thing as they did in high school (except that the objects of intrigue have changed to fraternities and bright futures in sales). Despite all this, it encourages me to know that the music is here, and it seems to be thriving.

Now the headlining band—the one I specifically came to see—will put on a great show, and afterwards I will get to meet them. But what strikes me most about the night is this moment, as I sit off to the side of the stage, observing in equal parts the crowd and the opening band. I am not hit with any revelation, but more a reassurance, a reminder of something that I've known all along. I see a girl in the crowd, dancing. But it is more than that. The way she moves. The look of serenity and pleasure on her face. There is something so graceful about her, so carefree and in the moment. Not like she has forgotten about her troubles, but as if her movements were the product of all the angst and frustration in the world leaving her body. This is powerful. Never before have I witnessed something so subtly, supplely, sublime.

She is dancing to music that someone like me created—music I know I can, and am on my way to creating. This is what our parents and those washed-up musicians recreate in this very building most nights. Music is more than just chords and melodies. It's more than shutting myself in my room and playing acoustic guitar, singing songs that were meant to be performed by one person, or even adapting songs so that they can be performed by one person. Music is social, it's a language. It's communion, and it's meant to be shared. Shared between the stage and the crowd are the collective memories and reactions of all those who play and hear it. I haven't been playing music, merely practicing it. Music is in the performance, and the chemistry of the four guys on a stage. It's in the power of a bass amp, the crack of a snare, and a mix that's too loud. It is youth and life without responsibility that our parents revisit when they sit down at the Iron Horse Music Hall. It is energy and motion and emotion, raw and unarticulated. Most of all, music is that girl in the crowd. Someday I will look out from the stage and see her and know that I have found it.

Dancing into the Light

ROBERT HAMMOND

From the first line of his essay, Hammond introduces the oppositional themes of "light" and "dark" and uses them throughout the essay both literally and figuratively. His small, isolated hometown and its almost total lack of light at night is in sharp contrast to his new home at UMass where he finally finds a place where he can begin to undertake a search for his identity. He embeds this quest within a narrative striking for its gender-neutral pronouns. Also note how Hammond becomes almost an outside observer, referring to himself in the second person "you" when reflecting on his thoughts and feelings.

Amherst is never dark. And it scares you.

There's a weird feeling in your stomach, the one where it feels like something is gnawing away at it, and it makes you sick. Your head is starting to pound right above the right temple. Your feet and knees are fine, however, and so you trail behind your friend as they twirl in their red skirt down the way.

"You should come dancing with me; it'll be fun, trust me!" they had said. You bought it with reflexive hesitance. But it's late, and they are walking out into town alone and planning on coming home alone as well. That's not something you allow. Your mom would be appalled to hear that you let a feminine-presenting person walk into a strange place alone at night and did nothing to stop or go with them for safety's sake. You nod, utter a quick agreement, plaster a smile on your face, and walk with them.

Amherst is never dark, and it's almost refreshing. Back at home, where everyone is literally related and from the same place, the streetlights don't work. Mile after mile is cloaked in darkness, with one solitary light every so often to break up the omnipresent dark. Back at home, where half of the area is woods or farmland, you couldn't go out at night. There's nothing there. The idea of having something worth doing at night is alien to you. It's refreshing, but also exhilarating. As you wander the brightly lit streets, the stores are open despite the fact that the sun has gone down.

The Masonic Lodge is a building you've never heard of or seen in your life before. Your stomach begins to wretch again, but you try to repress it. You recognize nobody inside. The fiddle plays and everyone moves like clockwork. Nothing is out of place, nobody trips or looks uncomfortable, and for just a moment it's like seeing the sun for the first time.

However, just like seeing the sun for the first time, you blink and the novelty is over; fear of the unknown replaces the human urge to explore and understand. Like a wounded animal, you dash out of the room at the earliest possible moment. This stomping ground is not yours.

Amherst is never dark, and neither is that room. It's brightly lit existence makes you tense, as if simply being there is causing all of your inadequacies to be brought to light.

Outside is still just as bright as the inside, however. Your friend wants you to learn how to dance. You blink once more, tilting your head. Dancing is not something you know how to do. You've only ever really attended a handful of dances in your life (school dances, all of them), and you always sat in the corner, head tilted in fascination and confusion at the mass of writhing teenagers on the dancefloor. The music you couldn't dance or sing along to was miasmic, threatening to shut you down. It's not like you had any desire to associate with any of the people there anyway. Their sneering faces and delicate but venomous tone when they spoke with you killed that desire at its roots.

But your friend gives you a look, the one where their lip quivers and their eyes widen and "c'mon, please?" comes out of their mouth and you just have to say yes. It's not like you can return home now. You've crossed a threshold, and you don't know how to go back.

Now, with practiced motions, your friend grabs your hand and leads you in the dance, and you trip, catching yourself on the cold pavement that leaves stones in your skin when you jump back to your feet. You laugh a bit, but less because you find your inherent clumsiness funny, and more because you'd rather not have your friend worry. Their face drops for a moment before you flash a smile (always the same, fake smile; the one everyone does back at home when people they don't like appear) that sets them at ease. They pull you back into the hall with renewed vigor, and within seconds and a "would you like this dance?" they've gotten themselves a partner to dance with, a tall, beardy sort of man who makes your friend look small and waifish in comparison. Everyone you ask to dance shrugs with an "I'm sitting this one out," or "I already have a partner for this one," and the gnawing in your stomach grows worse. You shrug to your friend, whose face is starting to wrinkle at their forehead in frustration.

You'll sit this one out, you say. It's fun to watch, you say. All things you have repeated to yourself for years now.

Now, they vanish. You wander over to the side. The sticky, humid air is threatening to make you pass out, and so you move to a seat in front of a fan, the cool night wind feeling like an Antarctic storm in comparison. Your head begins to pound more, pressure from behind your temples is making you want to lie down, but you stay alert and awake, and watch, just like you promised.

The hall is loud making your head feel more like an anvil than a limb, and everyone seems to know what they are doing. Basic fears jump into your head. What if you trip? What if you accidently punch someone? (You've done that before, many times.) What if nobody wants to dance with you and you've come all this way for nothing?

But then a sprightly girl makes her way over. You can't make out her name over the din of the dancing and the laughter and the fiddle. Maybe it's Mary? You don't have the slightest clue, but she can't make out your name through the sound barrier anyway, and so when the music stops and another dance begins, you allow her to lead you to the lines and attempt to pretend to know what you're doing.

Like a monster, the gnawing in your stomach threatens to knock you out flat, but you fight on like Beowulf against Grendel, one small man against seemingly impossible odds.

Back at home, this wouldn't have happened. With everybody knowing each other since birth (with the glaring exception of you, a foreigner), there was no blank slate. People you had never met knew your entire life story from their myriad webs of friends and cousins and second family members twice-removed, and you felt like you were cut off from that. To say it wasn't pretty is an understatement. But as the dance goes on, and you stumble and fall and occasionally are knocked to the floor by a well-meaning person trying to turn you in the right direction, you get a weird feeling of belonging.

When the dance ends, your friend finds you and ushers you out. Both of you are reeling with exhaustion, and you smile and put two thumbs up like you always do. Nobody died, right? So it must be a victory. And they smile.

"I'm proud of you," they say.

Amherst is never dark, and for once, you may be grateful.

Pages from a Diary Never Written

TANNER HOULE

Houle's first sentence tells us that "convention" does not suit his purpose, so we should not be surprised that his essay not only breaks with the conventions of standard essay form, but also breaks with the chronological nature of diary form as well. Making use of highly descriptive language, strong verbs, metaphor, and poetic devices, the author moves back and forth in time according to how various memories and sense impressions trigger thoughts critical to his context.

---

21 September 2013: It is an accepted convention that diaries are written chronologically, trudging from one calendar year to the next, recording the mundane alongside the extraordinary. But because life is lived forward and understood in retrospect, and because my need now, having left home for the first time in eighteen years, is to understand what *Home* means, I will write to you, dear diary, in violation of this convention.

But let us locate Home on the map first. Home to me is a landscape that I have known in the intimate grammar of familiarity: the fastest route from supermarket to cornfields, the best restaurants to get some food, and hidden trails through the woods. This place is Chelmsford, my hometown that I haven't been away from for a period longer than a week and a half—not until now. It's where the routine, the march of the everyday, year after year, gave my days their identity.

6 July 2004: A month before I turned ten, we were down on the Cape on our annual summer vacation. I couldn't resist rushing down the old, worn dirt path that cut through the woods and led to the ocean. I could always tell when I was close to meeting the beach: broken shells layered the ground, dropped by the seagulls that patrolled the sky, and the smell of the salty air and the light breeze always hit me. All I wished to do was to get to the jetty. I would spend hours on end with a small piece of meat attached to the tall piece of sea grass I plucked from the sand with one thing in mind: catching the crabs that sat hiding beneath the rocks. I was too young to tie the meat to the grass myself, and worried that the crafty crustacean would steal it, so I relied on my older brother and cousins to re-knot it—again and again. Finally, after calling it a day of crab catching, I would join my family at the chairs positioned in a half circle a few feet from the water. I only heard snatches of the family conversations—cementing, as always, around memories of summers prior, the Red Sox, or the evening plans—getting up constantly to collect the smooth, washed up rocks by the water's edge. I settled down when the baskets were opened and sandwiches, set on paper plates, were passed around. The outdoors filled with smells that had earlier filled our kitchen. The pebbles sitting in my pocket, taken from our garden, were to be offered to the ocean here. The rocks from here would be arranged on my window sill. The outdoors, I realized that day, is an extension of home. The boundaries of what Home can mean were in that moment pushed and widened.

12 September 2006: Middle school had just begun. My friends and I, excited at this academic recognition of our growing out of childhood, decided on meeting at the freshly cut baseball fields down the road from my house. We were the only ones there at that early hour, sitting in the bleachers and eating popped popcorn with a raspberry slush that colored our mouths blue. We were mimicking adults who often sat there when a game was on, arguing feverishly over a particular sports maneuver or brooding over a missed call. We were in no hurry to grow up; we *were* eager to be given the freedom adults are granted.

After the players who were practicing on the field left, we abandoned our popcorn and slush and took to the fields. The air buzzed with our voices as we participated in a competitive game of wall ball. In under an hour, though, we abandoned our game too and ran down the side-path to the corkboard that had just been updated with the sports stats of the players. Many of our ranks had risen up a rung. Our promotion to middle school and now this: a rare day when the hours were thick with windfalls, the sort that make you look at the future with eyes full of hope and excitement.

To celebrate, we decided on watching reruns of David Ortiz making game-winning homeruns on YouTube. Watching his winning streak was what first created a communal sense of excitement among us, turning us from teammates to friends. And to draw the night to a memorable close we did what was a reminder of the age we were trying to grow out of. We exchanged baseball cards.

When I got back home, I added my newly acquired cards to a stack that had grown from a single pack into a collection held together in four albums. They were all hidden behind clothes hanging in my closet, creating the thrill of a secret and also obscuring them from open scrutiny and from judgments that would perceive my hobby—and consequently me—as childish. It was a duality I was completely comfortable with, something that I saw as necessary to buy my inclusion into the adult word.

15 August 2013: The yearly neighborhood cookout took place at my house this summer. A splashing pool filled with the kids from our street and their screams could be heard over the music of Kenny Chesney and Jimmy Buffet playing out of the speakers that sat on the wooden bench—the electric cord uncoiled and stretched out to an indoor plug by the screen door. My friends and I went into my room and spoke about high school, our last four years in Chelmsford where the seasons were remembered by the games we played: the familiar heat of the Friday night lights of the football game in the fall; spring, the season of baseball, times of triumphant underdog wins as the earth around us struggled to shrug off the remnants of sun-melted snow, the season when I pitched my way to headlines in the Lowell Sun, Boston Herald, and online at ESPN Boston. While the knowledge of what it meant to be a local hero was heady, the brotherhood we shared as a team is what I would cherish when it was time for me to go. We appeared in each other's driveways late in the night, the sound of our car's engine buzzing through the quiet hour, a coded signal in response to which our friends would run out of the door to meet us. When we were low on gas, we would tap at the windowpane of our friend's room and take our discussions to the dimly lit back porch or pool, cicadas screeching in the background through the heady scent of crushed pinecones.

As I sat on the floor alongside my friends—the same ones who played with me on my baseball team when I was nine, whose houses I reached, running through the woods eight years later, seeking safety when a house party I was at got busted—I realized that there was a finality to this act of sitting together in my room. We may meet again over winter or summer break, we may reminisce about the times gone by, but the act of remembering will not be part of the sequence of our childhood. It will be removed: the memories in the past, the recollection in the present. We may look back and find more meaning in our past, but the sense of continuity would be broken that evening when the cookout ended. George Steiner once said that it is not our pasts, but the images of our past that rule us. Remembering, I realized, would become an act of submitting to images of the past and not an actively recorded experience.

Outside, the smell of sweet marinated chicken and tender steak thickened the air with a rich aroma. Someone was clapping in tune to a song. A stray bit of laughter made its way up through my window. An insistent clanking rose from the empty cans and bottles colliding in the bin. Voices started calling out our names. It was time to go.

30 August 2012: Now, at UMass, I am constantly surrounded by thousands of people I have never seen, walking around me, laughing or clapping each other on the back as I walk from one class to another. Clutching at the straps of my backpack, I think of Chelmsford nights when a small convoy of cars—music blaring, packed tight with friends—went through town. Now my room is smaller in what feels like a much larger world. There are new names to be learned, new landscapes to be discovered. I feel a glimmer of homesickness, not just for the physical spaces of my town but also for the space people carry: a corner where I would once nestle and find warmth after an evening of shoveling the snow outside our bricked front steps; a corner where family stories, with repeated telling, acquired the quality of a legend.

Everyone knows everyone else has been turned into a small town cliché, but it is the knowledge that shaped my hour: in Chelmsford I knew the fabric of every road, the exact places I could step on in the nighttime darkness without breaking the silence with the cracking of a twig; I knew the trails to lead you to silent, uninterrupted peace; the ponds and rivers that invited you to sit down and ponder with a fistful of pebbles, a rock offered to the water for each thought that resolved itself with satisfying click of clarity.

Do I know what home means? Maybe not. But I haven't abandoned my exploration. Here is an epiphany for you in the meanwhile: I'm now left with an expanded notion of 'playground': from being the yard of my house, it became the backstreets, parks, produce markets, and trails of Chelmsford.

23 August 2013: I began to recall memories from many of the things that really stood out to me from my past here in Chelmsford. The thoughts of walking with my dad through the old overgrown trails, past still ponds we had discovered heading towards the remnants of a lost car, eaten by ground, claimed by creepers, and beaten by countless winters. I don't remember any of our conversations. But I remember his voice. I remember thinking that his personality resonated throughout the intimate space of my hometown, or perhaps my hometown has inherited features from him—that was what made it so familiar. He and I played catch while waiting for my bus to school every day in elementary and middle school. He taught me how to fix my broken chain on my bicycle, and later, how to work on my truck. He walked me to the fields where I practiced, and every Sunday when I was fifteen, my father and I went to the huge vacant parking lots of big corporations, circles of tire tracks left in the sand, proof of the driving lessons he gave me.

My room, that evening, was emptied into backpacks and duffle bags and loaded into the truck—drawers emptied and yanked open, the desk top bare as I had never seen it, and an empty corner where a TV once sat. The room had relapsed to a state from a distant past. My childhood had at last drawn to a close, not in middle school, but now, on my last day in Chelmsford.

16 September 2013: I am warming up to my newfound independence and this opportunity of defining myself without supervision. As I buckle down to the academic and residential life at UMass, as I stumble upon faces that are turning gradually familiar in the dining hall or down the corridors of Thoreau, as friendships are formed over tales from *back home* and homework assignments, I think of Chelmsford, but with a sense of dull foreboding. I am no longer worried that I will turn sick remembering Chelmsford over and over. My worry is that I may forget; that someday time and distance and the euphoria of the newness and freedom would allow Chelmsford and all that it meant to slip away, leaving behind nothing but a washed down image that evokes no strong emotion, nothing more than a vague sense of nostalgia. Perhaps such indifference will only be temporary, if at all, and with time, my definition of home will only expand to include UMass and the friends I meet here? I don't know, and this is precisely why it's now—when both the past and present are fresh in my mind—that I should explore what Home means to me.

Coloring Outside the Lines

DANIEL KIELY, JR.

In "Coloring Outside the Lines," Daniel Kiely uses the idea of coloring within the lines—the main lesson he took away from his religious education classes— as an extended metaphor to explore the conflict between his seeking, spiritual self and his failing loyalty to the established dogma of his Roman Catholic church. Through a series of reflective narratives, each themed with appropriate lines from "The Lord's Prayer," Kiely uses a secular, conversational voice that is rich with irony and humor even as he explores his deep conflict in situating his spiritual identity.

Our Father, Who art in Heaven, hallowed be Thy name

The only thing that kept me from becoming a priest was believing in God. Without this crazy narcissist in the sky, I would have been a Theology major on my way to seminary. But of course the idea of God had to get in the way. Ever since I started learning the history and practices of the Church, it was my sole obsession in life. My formal religious education was through CCD, Confraternity of Christian Doctrine, at our local Catholic church. Most of these dreaded Wednesday night meetings were spent coloring pictures of Jesus and various animals, followed by vague talks about what we should believe as good Catholics. The most the volunteer teachers taught me about God was that He was extremely boring and in desperate need of followers who could color inside the lines. The older I grew in the Church, the more my view of the Catholic understanding of God seemed extremely accurate. Every Sunday I saw more of what coloring in the lines meant, and how much I resented it. My mind wondered how many people in the pews actually believed anything the teachers taught us. My half-finished, postmodern picture of the birth of Jesus certainly did not give me any answers.

Thy Kingdom come, Thy will be done on Earth as it is in Heaven

I fared much better in Mass than in my humdrum religious education. Sunday mornings were an adventure into the exotic, the otherworldly. The sanctuary of the church seemed gigantic, cavernous, even magical. It was the closest thing to Hogwarts my ten-year-old self could ever experience. Mass in the church engaged all my senses: incense burned, men in odd dresses waved their arms at marble tables, communion wafers left an aftertaste on my tongue, legs fell asleep sitting on wooden pews, but most of all, hymns were sung. All of these exercises of the senses combined in communal singing. The organ would burst out in its rich sound and parishioners would join voices, offering up their energy to a vague idea of God. There was no way to know what ideas the person next to you had about a higher power, but that did not change the fact that you were singing in unison with him. Mass was a playground where my ten-year-old mind could play with a sense of wonder—the transcendent God everyone seemed to talk about. Mass brought with it the inexplicable joy only available to children. These mystical experiences set me up for a lifelong journey of searching for the source of that connection I felt during Mass.

Although I felt at home in a church, I could not sort out my confusion about what this 'God' figure was. The curiosity to find my own answer emerged from the joy of worship, leading me to read every book or article I could about any religion in existence. My childhood reading and vocabulary were increased only because efficiency in this religious research was essential to my life's satisfaction. The reverent seed of religious practice slowly grew into a craving for information and the critical thinking to search for a better answer than the noncommittal mutterings of a volunteer CCD instructor.

Give us this day our daily bread, and forgive us our trespasses as we forgive those who trespass against us

Not all of my Catholic role models were from my home church. My great aunt took her novitiate, the first set of vows to become a Religious Sister, at the age of seventeen. She grew to become a compassionate woman whose virtues shaped my ideals of what a human can be. My religious inclination repurposed almost all of our family trips to her convent from social visits to scholarly pursuits inside the privacy of my mind. Here among the sisters the religious virtues I learned on Sundays were fully practiced. There was no priest droning on without any connection to the individuals he spoke to. The lifestyle felt much more like the connection of hymn singing than a bond of shared intellectual thought. I saw the same group of nuns from my birth until the passing of my great aunt this summer. They still remembered my name and small details about who I was as a person. Those women showed the most human beauty I have ever seen—all through their smiles and kind words. Submerging myself in Catholic religious life showed me the virtue of true compassion to others, and just how much I craved to practice it.

My observations at the Motherhouse informed the experiential side of my religious education. Compassion transformed into a daily practice in the lives of the nuns. In a secular imitation of this lifestyle, I try to look into a mirror every night. If my eyes have the same brightness of the nuns, I have met my goal of compassion for the day. If they are lackluster, I have to open myself up to a little more kindness. The Catholic theologian in me automatically recalls how wonderful a world filled with unique humans loved equally can be. The sparkle comes back to my eyes most nights. In this way, the fire of love living in those nuns lives inside of me—I just don't need to wear a habit to achieve it.

And lead us not into temptation, but deliver us from evil

When I was thirteen I had my first feelings for another man. No matter how liberal a parish, this always presents an obstacle. Even without believing in God, the morals of my religious upbringing came back to haunt me. These feelings made me feel stained. No sponge could scrub off the sinful cravings inside me. Ingrained in my mind was the true goal of Catholic life—a loving marriage. Two men did not fit this image. Two men could not, in the eyes of a God I did not believe in, experience love in the same way. Even without believing in this system I had become a member of it, enough to rebuke myself for something organic in origin. The weight of being outside the Catholic norm certainly created damage. My great aunt's compassion suddenly made me feel shameful. The exercise of compassion somehow seemed to end just short of myself. The internal struggle lasted until the present day. Sorting out the positive lessons from the negative is my new religious study. I gain strength by deciding what aspects of the vast body of Church practice and teaching are worth my personal investment.

No matter how un-Catholic my brain urges me to be, I cannot help the way my heart warms at the sight of a church. There is no fighting my natural reaction to fear being a prayer to the man I scribbled pictures of all those Sundays. Even larger than these knee-jerk reactions, Catholicism left an understanding of what it is to be a good person that is indestructible inside me. Somewhere in my bored pew sessions I absorbed a sense of morality, and maybe even a way to create my own lines to color within.

Amen.

Double Identity

BRIAN JAEHYUNG KIM

In "Double Identity," Brian Jaehyung Kim explores how he moves between two very different cultural identities. Kim begins his essay with a series of anecdotal flashbacks that rapidly engage the reader and create the context for his artful examination of times when he has thought of himself as Jaehyung—his given Korean name—and Brian—his adopted English name. Careful selection of details and vivid description immerse the reader in each of Kim's identities.

Amherst, Massachusetts: September 2014

The whole campus seemed to be in a rush. Movers were carrying boxes left and right; students were saying goodbyes to their families and hellos to their new roommates. As I stood in front of the door of what would become my new home, I frowned at the name that was stuck on the door: Jaehyung. I immediately put down my backpack, took out a pen and scribbled over the name tag. It no longer read Jaehyung, but instead had a new name: Brian.

Seoul, South Korea: March 2010

I was finally back in my home country after seven years in a foreign country. Was school here going to be as hard as the numerous tales had made it out to be? Was I going to have trouble fitting in? Was I going to survive the competition and the endless hours of studying that was required of every student in the country? I had no idea. All I knew was that I was ready for the challenge. As I got dressed in the newly purchased school uniform, I couldn't help but smile. I had always been disgusted at the idea of wearing a uniform to school, but it didn't look too bad. I put on the shirt, the jacket, and the dull gray pants. Finally, I pinned my name tag on the left side of my chest. The name tag read Jaehyung Kim. Or more accurately, 김재형.

Moscow, Russia: August 2002

"If you don't understand what they're saying, just say 'Pardon me?'" my mom reminded me as she helped me get on the bus. Today was the big day. Jaehyung Kim, a little boy who was born and raised in Korea for the past eight years of his life, was in another country, boarding a bus that would take him to a school that would speak another language. As the bus approached the school, I could read the sign: "Anglo American School of Moscow." I was going to meet kids from all over the world here, all united in one school, all speaking one language: English. As I found my way into the classroom and settled down, the teacher required us to take part in the usual, boring, introduce-yourself-to-the-class ordeal. However, I was excited. I was excited to set foot into a new school, excited to be surrounded by people from all across the globe, and excited to introduce myself to those people. When my turn came, I stood up, full of energy, and announced, "Hi, my name is Brian Kim!"

A name carries more meaning than a combination of letters you write on the top right portion of your test or a sequence of sounds that you respond to. A name is something that represents you and who you are. You can find out quite a bit about a person just by their name. For example, let's take my name: Brian. If Jake from Texas, the quintessential American college student, sees or hears my name, he can safely assume that I am also a male, as opposed to if he heard the name Brianna, in which case he would infer that I was a female. If Jake were to come across the name Jaehyung, he would know that I am from a different country than he is, for as of yet, to my limited knowledge, there have been not too many American babies named Jaehyung.

Just like that, a name can give out information such as one's gender and which region of the world one is from. In most cases, a name can guide you to find out information about someone before even meeting them. However, for me, my name can be misleading and misguiding. When Jake hears the name Brian, he might not immediately match it with a tall, black haired, Asian boy with glasses, and he might not assume right away that I was from the other side of the world. I have two names—Brian and Jaehyung—and I have two identities—Brian and Jaehyung.

Jaehyung was born in Korea. He comes back from school everyday. He eats dinner with his family and watches TV with them. On the weekends, he likes to play tennis with his dad. Jaehyung goes to Korea during vacations and visits his family. Every lunar New Year, he dresses up in formal, traditional Korean attire and performs the traditional bow to his grandparents, parents, uncles, and aunts, wishing them all a healthy and fruitful year. He speaks Korean, eats Korean food, and practices Korean culture. Jaehyung is Korean.

Brian was never born, but technically created. He goes to school every day. He eats lunch with his friends and enjoys playing sports with them. On the weekdays, he enjoys calling his friends for a game of basketball or a night at the movies. During the school year, Brian engages himself in his academics: participating in group projects, writing essays, and taking exams. He likes to take the train to Boston and walk around the city, exploring different shops and different restaurants. He speaks English, eats American food, and likes what American culture has to offer. Brian is American.

Brian will never visit his grandparents during the vacation and wear traditional Korean clothes. Brian does not speak Korean and does not practice the Korean culture. Whenever his friends ask him to teach them how to speak Korean, he laughs it off and tries to change the subject. When fellow Korean students approach him and try to start a conversation in Korean, he responds in English and tries his best to avoid them. Brian takes pride in the fact that he isn't like the "other Koreans" and that he "doesn't seem Korean at all." Whenever he and his non-Korean friends engage in a conversation about his home country, it would go something like:

"Do you listen to K-Pop?"

"No."

"Why do Korean people like to wear such tight-fitting clothes then?"

"I wouldn't know."

"But you're Korean?"

"Yeah, not really. Whatever."

Brian has always attended an international school where not many people were Korean. He is used to making friends with people who speak English, and it feels awkward to him and makes him uncomfortable when he has to become Korean in front of them. Brian isn't Korean. He doesn't know how to be, and he doesn't want to be.

Jaehyung will not present his group project to his classmates; he will not walk around the city of Boston, visiting shops and buying video games. Jaehyung does not speak English and does not endorse the American culture. Whenever he returns to Korea to visit his family, he is the center of attention. They crowd around him, asking what life is like in a foreign country. They ask him to say something in English, and are impressed when they find out that he can roll his "r's." Jaehyung understands that most of his family members are jealous of the fact that he is near-fluent in English—something every Korean wants these days. However, he feels alienated. He feels like they're treating him like someone from another planet, gathering around him and asking him to perform tricks that they cannot. Ever since he was born, Jaehyung has been raised in a Korean family, speaking Korean and practicing Korean culture. Jaehyung isn't American. He doesn't know how to be, and he doesn't want to be.

These two identities are both present in one body: me. I am both a Korean and an American. I speak their languages, understand and practice their cultures. Sometimes I'm Brian: English is the more comfortable language for me, I enjoy being American, and I want to be treated like other Americans. I don't want to stand out just because my looks suggest that I might be from another country. Other times, I'm Jaehyung. Korean is my native language, and I do everything a Korean would do. When I am with my family and my Korean friends, I want to fit in, to be one of them. I don't want to stand out because I know how to speak English or because I've spent time with people from all over the world. Did I prefer being one identity over the other? Not necessarily. However, when I was Brian, I wanted to be Brian. When I was Jaehyung, I wanted to be Jaehyung. But which one was the real me? Did I have to pick one over the other? Would one have to be the dominant identity and the other take the back seat? Was it even possible to live with two identities?

There was one little fact that I missed when I was struggling to find out which one was the real me. Both Brian and Jaehyung have the same last name: Kim. Both Brian and Jaehyung are in me: two seemingly different people sharing one body, taking turns to express themselves. At first it was confusing. It always seemed like I was in conflict with myself, unsure about who I was, until I realized that these two identities aren't in conflict, but coexisting in a certain harmony that only I can produce. Not many people in this world have the name Brian. Fewer people have the name Jaehyung, and even fewer people have both names. I am both Brian and Jaehyung. I am the tall, dark-haired, Asian boy who can be seen walking among a group of friends, laughing and pushing one another around. I am also the tall, dark-haired, Asian boy who can be seen sitting among his family members, dressed up nicely in traditional clothing, enjoying the sweetness of freshly sliced fruit. I am both Brian and Jaehyung Kim.

Interacting with Text

Preface

We often write to engage with the ideas of others, particularly in academic contexts. Because dialogue is at the heart of meaning-making in universities, *College Writing* asks students to "wrestle" with a published text in a unit called "Interacting with Text." Writing to an academic audience, students work to balance understanding and fair representation of the text (specifically: effective summary, paraphrase, quotation, and citation of a text) with a critical response. This begins the process of writing to more distant audiences—audiences that are broader than fellow classmates, family members, or friends—and to understand the kinds of thinking and writing valued by academic communities.

The "Interacting with Text" essays included here represent student interactions with the work of published writers. Drawing on their own histories and experiences, these student writers place their own perspectives in dialogue with those of a published writer. The challenge is, at once, to contemplate the sophisticated ideas shared by professional authors in the course's reader and to present one's own perspective on those ideas: for example, to re-think one's perspective on the topic, to apply a writer's claims to a different context, to tease apart the nuances of a writer's assertions, to re-define a key concept in an essay, and more. To understand these writers' ways of responding, we might imagine how the writers of the "Inquiring into Self" essays, based on their personal contexts, might have responded differently to the issues presented in this section.

Photos May Disappear, but Memory Never Dies

NADJA ARIFOVIC

Nadja Arifovic's response to Susan Sontag's essay on war photographs resonates with personal voice, powerfully moving description, and real-life narratives conveyed to her by her parents who witnessed first-hand the atrocities of the Bosnian war. Arifovic's seamless inclusion of quotes and summaries from Sontag's piece contributes to a feeling of continuous immersion in her essay, even as she tempers Sontag's argument that war photos cannot be understood without a narrative.

At first glance, the photo appears to look normal: lush, green rolling hills dotted with burnt orange roofs peeking out from behind emerald trees. Yet your eyes are drawn to the center of the image where there's a blanket of white masking the summer-green hues. The severe contrast of the white on green makes it look as if winter's chill paid a visit to the summer's day, covering the valley with snow. The white mass remains a beautiful mystery from a distance and stays as such until you examine the image further. The first thing you notice is the sea of uniform, white-stone slabs lining the field. They stretch in an almost dizzying fashion across acres of land, something rather unbelievable and oddly captivating. The image stays ingrained in your mind when you blink and you can't understand why the thought of it fills you with dread. Only when you learn that these are the gravestones of the thousands lost in the bloody Bosnian War do you feel a wave of sickness pass over you.

After seeing the image, my mind never fails to conjure this haunting scene when I think of Sarajevo. Deep inside, I've come to recognize that even with the beautiful brick buildings and lovely people, the white gravestones are what make the city what it is today. With each person who was killed by the bombs and bullets, a small part of Bosnia died as well; the gravestones are there to keep the memory of these people alive, a monument that defines Bosnia today.

Beyond the gravestones found in the abandoned Olympic stadium in Sarajevo, there are many grim reminders of the event that shook the small country of Bosnia in the 1990s. Houses with bullet holes are scattered across the country, buildings in ruin accent empty fields, and rusty signs hang from old chains, bearing warnings of land mines beyond them. The horrors of war can be found everywhere you look in Bosnia through landmarks that were blasted into existence in the middle of a village or city. If you travel to Sarajevo, you'll notice a war museum sits in the middle of the city, yet another reminder of Bosnia's dark past. Images of these remnants of war can be found with the click of a mouse and a quick Google search, or in written accounts of survivors. Regardless of where the image is found, the effect is the same: the photos evoke a sense of humanity and hurt.

In her essay, "Regarding the Pain of Others," Susan Sontag speaks about the power of war photographs to keep memory alive. "People want to be able to visit—and refresh—their memories" (Sontag 262). In Bosnia's case, the countless remnants of the war play an essential part in our attempt to come to terms with the senseless tragedies that shook the nation. Though Sontag claims that people have the need to revisit memories, the opposite can also be true, especially when it involves painful remembrances of war and death. People, however, *need* to refresh their memories. Regardless of the amount of pain a memory may cause, keeping it alive is crucial to the survival of the event itself, whether it is to learn from its atrocities or to honor those we lost. "Photographs of the suffering and martyrdom of a people are more than reminders of death, of failure, of victimization. They invoke the miracle of survival" (262). We can look to these photos for strength and hope, as they remind us of what we have overcome.

Coming from a Bosnian refugee family, I see firsthand how painful it is when my parents are reminded of the war in Bosnia. Words alone hold enough power to provoke a reaction from many Bosnians who fled the war. When discussing war of any kind, my parents instantly tense up; my mother's eyes become glossy and wide, and through them I see the hardship she's endured. I still recall the story of my mother's close college friend, an amicable, portly man who smiled a lot. They would call him *Buco*, a lighthearted name that meant "chubs." One day he was brought out of his house, along with his father and brothers, and was shot on the doorstep.

Photos bring out a side of my parents they wish to conceal from view: the horrid memories of leaving everything behind, sounds of bombs dropping, or news that their friends had been shot in their yards by Serbian soldiers. Sontag says, "To remember is, more and more, not to recall a story but to be able to call up a picture" (263). The reverse can be argued also, as an image may spark a memory of a story to arise instead. In addition, for a war victim, the picture recalled may not be of a single photo. To outsiders, or non-victims, war "photographs lay down routes of reference, and serve as totems of causes: sentiment is more likely to crystallize around a photograph than around a verbal slogan" (261). If a Bosnian victim were to tell a story to someone unaffected by the war, only some sympathy would be triggered within the listeners. However, if a photo was shown to that person instead, they would have something to directly link them to the war and give at least a glimpse into the horrors of conflict. Although not as effective as having the memory of the war embedded in one's mind, photos are nearly powerful enough to evoke the feelings that war victims must deal with each day. The photos from the Bosnian war are not free of blood and death but rather the opposite, as are many war photos. After all, "…this posthumous reality is often the keenest of summations" (261) in terms of evidence of war atrocities. By seeing depictions of dark images of the conflict, whether of moments of combat or after a gruesome event, people can better connect and believe that what happened in the war was truly terrible. Common memories in the form of photos bring people together and help establish a sense of community, which in turn relieves the pain that war victims and their families may experience.

Ron Haviv, a photojournalist, documented the Balkan wars and the atrocities that occurred during them. His most famous photograph depicts a Serbian soldier kicking an old woman lying on the ground between two bodies. Sontag states that "in fact, the photograph tells us very little—except that war is hell, and that graceful young men with guns are capable of kicking overweight older women lying helpless, or already killed, in the head" (263).

I don't agree that the photo tells very little. Maybe in terms of specific context, but as a Bosnian, the photo tells me everything I need to know and more. From stories told by relatives, I know of the horrors and inhumane treatment of the Muslims in Bosnia. The photo sparks a shock in me, yet those who have not been exposed to anything related to the war may not understand the significance of the photo; these may be the type of people Sontag is referring to in terms of "not knowing" what the photo is about.

Another, more powerful image that stays with me is a photo of a man with his hands propping him up, a look on his face as if he was watching the whole world burn before his eyes. A soldier stands behind him with a gun held ready. The story of my mom's friend being murdered in his yard was enough to tell me what was happening in the image. The man, no doubt a Muslim, was begging for his life, about to be killed by a Serb. To an outsider, this picture may mean little without the caption, but to Bosnians, its meaning is vivid. I may have not been in the war, but I cannot bring myself to look at the photo with dry eyes. The importance of these images doesn't lie in the fact that they cause emotion; it lies in the fact that the memory of the war and impact of the genocide, no matter the form, is made fresh again.

Memory should never be extinguished, and photos are an almost tangible way of reliving the past. By remembering the Bosnian War, the pain of it all brings people together; it prevents the past from repeating itself and it helps to keep the lessons from the war alive today, at least in the mind. Personal narratives are, in a sense, more powerful than photos. Pictures are a fairly new invention in history; the reason we know so much about the past is because, at the time, stories and words were all that was needed to express an idea or describe an event. Photos can tell parts of a story, but they can never give the full details of it, nor can they make you shiver when the speaker's voice trembles while telling the tale; photos can aid in expressing a thought, but can never provide full context. However, with the help of photos, memories will forever remain fresh so that the stories of those who lie beneath the snow-white tombstones in Bosnia's countryside will never be forgotten.

Work Cited

Sontag, Susan. "Regarding the Pain of Others." *Other Words: A Writer's Reader.* Eds. David Fleming et al. Dubuque: Kendall Hunt, 2009. 257–265. Print.

Feminization, Education, Masculinity: A Response to Michael S. Kimmel

ANDY MARTON

Between the epigrammatic quotes that structure his essay and a distinctive voice that is all his own, Andy Marton illustrates how to respond fairly to another author while making an original argument in a unique framework. Marton represents Kimmel's points without losing his own voice among the quotes. Rather, he extends Kimmel's points while testing them against his own experiences in high school, with family, and in his personal relationships.

Because there is very little honor left in American life, there is a certain built-in tendency to destroy masculinity in American men.
—**Norman Mailer**

In, "'What About the Boys?' What the Current Debates Tell Us—and Don't Tell Us—About Boys in School," Michael S. Kimmel cites the statistic that boys "commit suicide four times more often than girls; they get into fights twice as often; they murder ten times more frequently and are 15 times more likely to be the victims of a violent crime" (91–92). His article examines why we have these disturbing figures. After reading his essay and reflecting upon my own experiences as a boy, I came to a conclusion similar to his: that boys in America are being trained with too much machismo that separates our "manliness" from our humanity.

Let's start with the claim that boys are being feminized. It sounds like this: in a world of political correctness and feminine idealism run amok, there is nowhere left for boys to assert their natural manliness and aggression. They're forced to act against their instincts, and the frustration of this unnatural abomination builds up with no healthy outlet for them. Kimmel rejects this idea by stating that it "creates a false opposition between girls and boys" (94). By arguing about why boys are so out of control, how they're neglected, we make the false assumption that girls and boys are completely different creatures and that there is nothing they have in common, an idea that Kimmel calls insulting (106).

I agree with Kimmel. Feminism has always been challenged, and its critics are willing to pervert it to re-assert male dominance. Reading Kimmel's portrayal of these arguments, I get from anti-feminist critics a call to return to the days where "men could be men" and women "knew their place," perhaps as docile housewives. I grew uncomfortable reading these arguments because they made me feel that women and girls are the enemy, the eternal yin to our yang, a force to be diminished. They didn't make me feel that women are human beings.

Having your adolescence at an all-male boarding school is just crap.
—Benedict Cumberbatch

This brings me to the conflict over single-sex education. If we accept the idea that boys and girls are irreconcilably different, then it seems reasonable to explore the option of creating schools for boys and schools for girls. It does seem, on the face of things, like an ideal arrangement. In my junior year of high school, I barely scraped by with a 'C' for the year in physics because I took it with my then-girlfriend. I didn't focus, and we'd sometimes sneak out of the class for a while. It would be easy to make the argument that I would have done better academically in an all-boys school.

Kimmel rejects this idea. He asserts that "women's colleges may constitute a challenge to gender inequality, while men's colleges reproduce that inequality" (102). In short, men are taught that women are inferior to them because where are the women to say otherwise? Kimmel also declares that "single-sex education for women often perpetuates detrimental attitudes and stereotypes about women" (103). Essentially, these colleges reinforce gender stereotypes. One of my friends goes to the all-female Smith College, which is known for its liberal arts education, as is Mount Holyoke. Meanwhile, the very math-and-science based schools are heavily male. CalTech reported 65% of incoming students in 2013 were male, and M.I.T. reported that in 2014 55% of those admitted were male.

I, however, think single-sex colleges are more an effect of stereotyping rather than a cause; by the time students get to college, gender seems to have divided students on school subjects. According to the article, high school boys tended to list science and math as their favorite subjects, while girls listed the humanities, citing their genders as reasons why (Kimmel 101). Math is a "male subject" because it's concrete, while English, where there is no one right answer, and everyone is free to share various thoughts, feelings, and interpretations, is seen as feminine. It's easier to reinforce stereotypes about what subject goes with what gender when the boys and girls are kept apart from each other.

I have two observations about separate-sex facilities to add to Kimmel's. The first is that arguments for these facilities are rooted in the idea that everyone is heterosexual. Some estimates conclude that ten percent of the population—which is not negligible—is homosexual. They are not being served by a school that is supposed to take dating pressures away from them.

The other observation I had was that whatever problems men seem to have interacting with women (and vice-versa) are just that, problems. The answer isn't separating boys and girls because we distract each other. That's not how life works. Dealing with the opposite sex is a learned ability. I stated before that because I took physics with my girlfriend, I got a "C" for the year. Dating a classmate doesn't justify a bad grade. My dad (who married his high school sweetheart) was furious when I tried to make that my excuse. If there really is such a problem between boys and girls regarding how they interact around each other, however, then it's better to teach in school how to resolve that tension rather than to increase it. I'm convinced that single-sex schools do the latter, exacerbating this supposed rift rather than healing it.

Boys will be boys—Unknown (common expression)

So feminization isn't the problem. Coeducational schools aren't the problem. What is the problem? Could it be cultural? Could it be biological? Why is it, as Kimmel points out, that "few European nations would boast of such violent, homophobic, and misogynist adolescent males" (99–100), while the U.S. has all these scary statistics? I've grown up always hearing that boys are just like that naturally—they just normally lean towards aggression and violence. It's biological. Our testosterone just makes us want to run around, hit things, act "like a boy." But aggression is not biological or hereditary. Kimmel cites a study from Stanford that shows that testosterone "doesn't cause it [aggression], but it does facilitate and enable the aggression that's already there" (96). So, aggression has to come from somewhere else.

I've always thought it to be cultural. In America, we're bombarded with aggression and violence. Football is one of the most popular games in American culture. Our superheroes use their might to beat up or kill the bad guys. All of us are taught the basic "boy code" that Kimmel summarizes in the essay: don't be a sissy (I heard that one a lot growing up), fight to be in charge, and take risks (99). I don't know why in America we have such a focus on boys having to act like this. Or why it's encouraged. Whenever I got too rowdy or aggressive, or too macho (my parents' favorite word when I exhibited a bit too much of this behavior), my mother's first words were always, "Don't be a dumbass." She and my father always say that this need for aggression to prove how manly you are is stupid, especially when it results in games like "Flinch" that Kimmel describes (105).

Not only is it stupid, it's dangerous. Part of childhood is learning control. It's not necessarily a good thing when a boy is aggressive. The right response is to find better ways of channeling, not encouraging these feelings, as therapist Michael Gurian would have us do (Kimmel 107).

I attended Wayland High School, which, in 2011, underwent a serious tragedy. We had a student at my school who had always been aggressive and violent. He played football and was very good at it. Once in a while, he was known to have a violent outburst or a tantrum, but hey, what boy doesn't lose his temper once in a while? When his girlfriend broke up with him, he was upset, but he didn't share his feelings. Why would he? That's sissy stuff. The summer after they graduated, he brutally beat his former girlfriend and strangled her to death with a Bungee cord. He's currently in prison serving life without parole. But the most chilling part of this story is that everyone was shocked he could do this. Why? "Well, sure, he had a temper, but that's just normal." While he is responsible for what he did, isn't it possible that not encouraging violence and aggression in boys the way our culture does could have prevented this young woman's tragic death?

I'm not just a boy toy. I have feelings and dreams like anybody else.

—Jon Stewart

This quote highlights my overall point. The problem isn't that boys' natural aggression is being held back; it's that we live in a society where boys have this culture of "manliness" thrust upon them very early in their lives that's so unhealthy. I feel bombarded all the time with the cultural need to prove my dominance over other men, and especially over women. That's a sentiment that I find to be deeply harmful.

I could spend several more pages talking about possible sources for boys' aggression—abusive fathers, our media, fear of being perceived as gay, Freudian penis envy—but it doesn't matter. We know that there is some problem with boys when they murder, commit suicide, drop out, and suffer from depression at staggering rates. As we've seen, I reject the idea that feminism or coeducation has caused these problems. In fact, my argument lies in that both are good things. Growing up, we all (boys and girls) need to be encouraged to become human beings: good people who don't need to use violence to express themselves, who aren't afraid to show emotion at appropriate moments. Kimmel ends his essay with this declaration: "Feminists also seem to believe the outrageous proposition that, if given enough love, compassion, and support, boys—as well as men—can also be people. That's a vision of boyhood I believe is worth fighting for" (107). I couldn't agree more.

Works Cited

"2013 Incoming Class Profile." *CalTech Undergraduate Admissions*. n.d. Web. 04 Oct. 2013.

Kimmel, Michael S. "'What About the Boys?' What the Current Debates Tell Us—And Don't Tell Us—About Boys in School." *Other Words: A Writer's Reader*. Eds. David Fleming et al. Dubuque: Kendall Hunt, 2009. 91–110. Print.

"Massachusetts Institute of Technology." *US News & World Report*. n.d. Web. 04 Oct. 2013.

Cultural Soup, à la American

WILLIAM McCARTHY

Does America swallow immigrants' culture whole when they join American society or does it celebrate diversity—just as long as that diversity keeps to itself? These are Richard Rodriguez's key views of how Americans deal with cultural assimilation in his essay "The North American." McCarthy uses the longstanding metaphor of America as a melting pot to respond to Rodriguez and offers an option he finds preferable. He extends the melting pot metaphor and fills it with his own alternative vision of a "cultural soup" he regards as palatable to all, thus concretizing the complex arguments made by Rodriguez. McCarthy's response is admirable for his fair treatment of Rodriguez's views and his constant engagement with the text.

From the beginning of our nation's history, the United States has expanded and grown because it was a nation of immigrants, a notion that I firmly believe still continues to this day. Beginning with English colonizers in the seventeenth century and throughout the next four hundred years, millions of people from all over the world came to America to have the opportunity for a better life. As citizens in this country, we often pride ourselves on being labeled a country that is a melting pot, where all these people and their cultures come together to form one great and expansive society. But an issue presents itself: if we were to look closely inside that "pot," how would we describe the soup of cultures that we see? Would we see, for example, a pot of pure chicken broth, one dominant ingredient taking up the whole pot? Or would we see a soup that is highly diverse in its ingredients yet with no mixing of those ingredients—a soup clearly created with defined sections within the whole? If this metaphor is equated to culture, asking these questions forces us to look at culture in the U.S. and how it affects or is affected by the immigrants who come here. Does "American" culture overpower their own once they arrive here, or does each of the different immigrant groups retain and separate themselves by culture? I believe the case can be made that both of these scenarios currently exist.

In his essay "The North American," author Richard Rodriguez presents the notion that the United States swallows immigrants and their cultures (227). He makes the case that this country and its culture has always swallowed the immigrants that come here and has essentially "Americanized" them—a term I hear thrown around a lot in public discussions on immigration. This notion would be the "soup broth" model of the cultural melting pot; some people in this country believe that all immigrant cultures have submitted and should continue to submit to American culture when they come here. Or, as Rodriguez puts it, "our national culture has been omnivorous" to arriving immigrants (227). I can see the impact this country has on immigrants by looking no further than my own family. My grandmother immigrated to this country from Germany when she was younger, and over the years she adopted the English language and many American customs. However, I find it hard to accept the notion of American cultural suppression on arriving cultures as something that always occurs. If all immigrants become totally "Americanized" during their time here, why does my grandmother still speak fluent German and watch European soccer? This example begs the question—is it feasible, or even ethical, for established Americans to ask immigrants to forget every characteristic of their own cultures, characteristics that are an essential part of their identities, and suddenly fit into the mold of people that are already here? I do not think that most immigrants discard every aspect of their former culture, and therefore Rodriguez's notion of what is happening with culture in the U.S. cannot be true all of the time.

Now we have to look at the other notion of culture in the U.S. that Rodriguez touches upon: that the U.S. is, and should be, a country that values every sub-culture equally, but with no intermixing. Rodriguez describes this notion of culture as "Canadian Multiculturalism" (228). Previously, without giving much thought to the topic, I always considered multiculturalism a good thing because it suggests that as a society, we value and respect all the different cultures within our country. However, in his essay Rodriguez shows the dangerous illusion that is created when we claim that we are a multicultural society. He says Americans can speak easily about diversity, but only to the point that they do not want to deal with or be involved with those in different cultural groups, or as he put it: "we are separate, our elbows do not have to touch, much less merge" (228). I agree with the logical leap that he makes. Americans claim we are diverse, but we are often hypocritical. It is true that for a very long time "race mixture has not been a point of pride in the United States" (Rodriguez 228).

The larger argument presented is that the desire to create a multicultural society for immigrants only creates fragmented cultural groups. This would be the thick soup model I presented earlier, and this reality creates a lack of interchange among cultural groups. This separation inevitably leads to tension between these groups, as Rodriguez shows by bringing up the 1992 L.A. race riots that demonstrated what happens when cultural groups in the U.S live in such close proximity to each other without interaction or respect (232). I find that this multicultural notion of the United States is not desirable or even representative of what happens between the various cultures within our borders. Therefore there must be a more accurate way to define this situation.

Regarding my soup in a melting pot metaphor, I realize now that I did not give many options for a viewer of this pot to choose from. I only described the extremes of the types of soup that could be in the pot. What if the soup in the pot just looked like regular chicken noodle soup, for instance? You've still got a good amount of broth, but you also have all the other ingredients mixed in as well. And every time you take a ladleful, you'll get something a little bit different from the last because the ingredients mix together in such a way that your perspective on what is in the soup changes every time. This is what I believe to be the best parallel for the relationship between American and immigrant culture. As Rodriguez describes it, "Culture is fluid. Culture is smoke in the air. You breathe it. You eat it" (234). In synthesizing the points Rodriguez makes in his essay, the case is made that both scenarios (cultural swallowing and multiculturalism) can occur, and have been occurring at the same time, which explains the diverse culture of the United States. This perspective makes it hard to objectively look at the cultural picture in the U.S. and not admit that there is mixing or overlapping between established American culture and these new immigrant cultures. I agree with this perspective. To espouse the belief that one of these scenarios is the only truth without recognizing that the other takes place as well is not a fair observation of the current system. This does not mean that one has to support both notions. Rodriguez conveys that both naturally occur at the same time: "If I had a bumper sticker, it would read something like ASSIMILATION HAPPENS. [...] I'm in favor of assimilation. I'm not in favor of assimilation. I recognize that it exists" (234). I believe that there needs to be a widespread recognition by people in this country that in an ideal world, neither of these scenarios exist by themselves; immigrants come and adopt aspects of American culture, but they also bring aspects of their own cultures to diversify and add to an established society.

There are many aspects of American society that highlight this interchange. One of the primary aspects of a culture is food, and I feel that I don't often stop and think about what cultural influences are behind the food I am currently eating. Hot dogs, pasta, pizza, sushi, and burritos are just a few examples of foreign cultural staples that have become central to the American diet. Holidays and cultural traditions are another example of the cultural exchange in this country. While immigrants will come to celebrate or recognize established holidays and traditions already celebrated here, many will also bring their own traditional customs as well. Over time, as people from outside those cultural groups come to celebrate those holidays and traditions as well, those events become an established part of regional and American cultural experiences, as is the case with Saint Patrick's Day, Mardi Gras, and Cinco de Mayo.

Rodriguez gives his own perspective on cultural exchange as well, examining the cultural diffusion between the U.S and his ancestral Mexico. He claims, "Northern Mexico looks like San Diego these days. [...] Everybody wants to be an American in northern Mexico. And South Texas is becoming very Mexican" (Rodriguez 231). What this shows is that each culture is changing and adding certain aspects to the other, especially in the areas of food, economy, and music. Rodriguez doesn't pick favorites, saying he can be a part of and value any culture that he wants to, whether it is Hispanic, American, or Chinese (234). What he tries to show is that people do not always have to be defined by the culture they are born into since culture is fluid and always changing. The value of intermingling cultures seemed to be absent from many Americans' societal ideals for a long time. Yet, as we continue to become a more interconnected and global world, the attitudes and mindsets of the people in this country are gradually evolving. The next generation seems to be more open to relationships between people of different cultures and races. Pew Research Polling shows millennials almost unanimously support interracial dating and marriages. The polling also showed that much of the younger generation has at least one friend that was of a different race or ethnicity (Pew Research Center). This suggests that the current generation understands, accepts, and values different backgrounds and cultures much more than older generations. I see this attitude being applied to newer immigrant populations as more and more people recognize and become interconnected with new cultures. I think this is important because there is a distinction between simply adopting aspects of another culture and actually valuing them, which the polling suggests this generation is more willing to do. In doing so, this country will continue to move towards achieving Rodriguez's goal of being a country with a strong appreciation, acceptance, and intermingling of different cultures.

The descendants of immigrants who have made the journey to this country have contributed so much to its cultural and social prosperity. But if we are to accept that, it is important to recognize that the outside cultural influences those immigrants have brought along the way have led us to where we are as a country today. Like Rodriguez, citizens of this country need to accept that both of those melting pot soups are happening at the same time because while America clearly changes the people that immigrate here, those very people change America as well. As our country continues to deal with and work through issues with our immigration system, I feel that it is essential for this reality to be accepted in order to solve some of these problems. We owe it to ourselves, and we also owe it to the immigrants who are "bringing America to America" (Rodriguez 233).

Works Cited

"Almost All Millennials Accept Interracial Dating and Marriage." *Pew Research Center.* Pew Research Center, 31 Jan. 2010. Web. 23 Feb. 2015.

Rodriguez, Richard. "The North American." *Other Words: A Writer's Reader.* Eds. David Fleming et al. Dubuque: Kendall Hunt, 2009. 227–235. Print.

Dissecting Our Sense of Justice

PETER SCAPICCHIO

Peter Scapicchio approaches Susan Sontag's essay, "Regarding the Pain of Others," by leading his readers through a series of ethical questions regarding their responses to war photographs. Using primarily a logical appeal, he employs careful deduction and an emotionally detached voice as rhetorical devices to discuss images that evoke strong emotions, making his writing both engrossing and provocative.

It is commonplace for someone to assume that their moral compass points 'true North' so to speak, but knowing what should be right, as well as what should be wrong, can often shock us when we discover what exists in actuality. In general, we tend to assume violence is bad, that war is unacceptable. In her essay "Regarding the Pain of Others," Susan Sontag affirms that the modern day approach is "the conviction that war is an aberration" (257). When we look at a photograph of a war atrocity, or a war photo in general, the common reaction is a feeling of sadness. We correctly relate war to death and loss. However, certain war photos possess the power to make us feel the opposite way. In an old World War II photo, we can see a man holding a Nazi soldier, who has his hands up in the air, at gunpoint. Information about this picture tells us that the man holding the weapon is a Jewish man, a prisoner held in a concentration camp, now freed by a successful attack by allied troops. Unsurprisingly, when someone looks upon this picture, they are fine with it. It seems to convey none of Sontag's "Uglifying, showing something at its worst" (260). In fact, some may see it is as inspiring, a triumph of good over evil. If you grind it down to a personal level, people see it as affirmation that their ideals are correct. But by grinding it down even more, right to the core, one must accept that this picture is, undoubtedly, the picture of a man pointing a gun at another man.

Should we, as morally decent Americans, attempt to be critical of photos such as these? Does thinking that this photo contains nothing offensive mean we are irrationally biased? Sontag tells us that we may be acting a bit high and mighty, reminding us that "Americans prefer to picture the evil that was *there,* and from which the United States—a unique nation, one without any certifiably wicked leaders throughout its entire history—is exempt" (262). We feel so far away from the people that could have committed the atrocities of the Holocaust, both morally and physically, that perhaps some deeply implanted part of our mind feels rewarded for approving of the picture. After all, it tells us the wicked are punished for their crimes, and the weak will throw off their oppressors. There is certainly some element of an inspiring message. However, we may be inflating the situation. It is no coincidence that the Nazi soldier's left arm faces us, the one with the iconic armband. The photographer wants us to see him as a Nazi, separate from us, separate from the man holding the gun to him, and certainly separate from our morals. At this point, we can take on the near-impossible task of ripping his armband off and judging him as one person, rather than one Nazi soldier. We can consider him a monster, or consider Sontag's possibility that he is "the reflection of a belief system, racism, that by defining one people as less human than another legitimates torture and murder," or perhaps someone who was "just doing what everyone else is doing" (264). By this logic, perhaps we cannot judge either party in the picture simply from their groups and appearances.

Is it not, however, appropriate for someone who is wronged in an atrocity to desire, and based on the extent of the wrongs, be allotted a payment of revenge? Even if it were for just a moment, the prisoner having power over his former captor seems like an appropriate payment for wrongs committed. This is justice in its most basic form, surely, an eye for an eye, and hardly a draconian punishment. Perhaps this prisoner had a personal vendetta against this soldier, or perhaps he had never seen him before. Would this revenge seem wrong if they had no prior relationship? Would it be right if they had?

Unfortunately, thinking this way may be peeling away that ignorance that we have tried so hard to hide. Sontag tells us "war has been the norm, and peace the exception" (257); it is thinking that we are entitled to revenge that has led to many wars over the course of civilization, and World War II was no exception to this rule. It seems as if justice must be meted out with care if progress is to be made towards peace.

Though Sontag might tell us that we should look at ourselves before judging others, it is more important to look at these photos, see the horrors that have been committed, and rather than remembering all the evils we have participated in, commit to learning the most important lesson that a horrid photo or any history lesson could ever teach us. The most important lesson in Sontag's examples—or the photo referenced in this paper—is that we look at these images as a warning. We see atrocities in progress, or in their aftermath, and while Sontag tells us the many effects they might have, we must look outside our wrongs, and look instead at the lesson for humanity as a whole. The lesson is simply that when we have this evidence, this clear horror produced by atrocity and the absolute proof that it happened, we must all resolve that it must never happen again. Though war is the norm, and atrocities will inevitably occur, we must document them, photograph them, and—no matter who the violator was—we must drill the lesson into our collective human consciousness. It is our duty to ourselves to know that we are capable of horrible things, and that we must always work to make sure such things never happen again.

Work Cited

Sontag, Susan. "Regarding the Pain of Others." *Other Words: A Writer's Reader.* Eds. David Fleming et al. Dubuque: Kendall Hunt, 2009. 257–265. Print.

Anger and Accountability in Antigua

ZOE SHENK

Shenk's essay is notable for both its incisive recognition and understanding of Jamaica Kincaid's forceful rhetorical choices in "A Small Place." Her introduction, initially framed as a critique of Kincaid's voice, catches Shenk's reader off guard for the rhetorical defense she later mounts in her essay. Shenk mimics Kincaid's use of second-person narrative as well as other rhetorical strategies not only as rhetorical analysis but also as a means to persuade her readers to recognize the truth of Kincaid's views.

In her essay, "A Small Place," Jamaica Kincaid creates an unquestionably powerful and provocative critique of the exploitive tourism industry in her native Antigua. However, by specifically targeting the privileged visiting tourists who perpetuate the oppressive power structure of postcolonial tourism, Kincaid risks losing her intended audience—those same people—entirely. Despite the danger, Kincaid masterfully walks that fine line between education and alienation in order to give us the rude awakening we deserve and require.

From the very first paragraph, it quickly becomes evident that Kincaid is on the offensive. You may initially think, as I did, that being from a tourist-infested, New England beach town lends you a certain level of expertise on the subject of tourism. Divorce yourself from these notions. Kincaid makes it very clear that *you* are the person under her microscope: "you are a tourist, a North American or European—to be frank, white—and not an Antiguan black" (111). As a tourist on a whirlwind tour of Antigua, Kincaid controls your every thought and punctuates each one with a jab about your abundant privilege and ignorance. When you note the beautiful sunny weather, Kincaid coos bitterly, "Since you are on your holiday, since you are a tourist, the thought of what it might be like for someone who had to live day in, day out in a place that suffers constantly from drought…must never cross your mind" (111). When you breeze through customs on your way to your hotel, Kincaid is there to explain:

> You are a tourist…and not an Antiguan black returning to Antigua from
> Europe or North America with cardboard boxes of much needed cheap
> clothes and food for relatives, you move through customs swiftly, you
> move through customs with ease. Your bags are not searched. (111)

Every detail you notice about the island, from the mansions of corrupt politi-
cians that line the poorly paved streets to the poorly maintained Japanese cars
that fill them, is twisted to illustrate the sheer magnitude of your ignorance.
By referring to the reader as *you* and writing in the second person, Kincaid is
able to force her readers to be accountable; she disallows readers from distanc-
ing themselves from their own problematic, ugly behavior.

Even the sprawling structure of the essay itself, while perhaps difficult on
the eyes, is extremely deliberate. Because Kincaid's intended audience is not
inclined to consider her argument in the first place, she forcibly silences readers by providing very few paragraph breaks. This manipulation allows for
fewer opportunities for interjection and protest by the audience. Even the
most hostile of readers has no choice but to go along for the ride, so to speak.

While Kincaid uses second person narrative and paragraph length to effectively implicate her readers, she does so at the expense of potentially being
perceived as accusatory. Overwhelmed by discomfort, it is easy to see how you
could feel personally attacked. You feel insulted, mocked, and unable to get
a word in edgewise by design. Kincaid uses a lot of sarcasm, which borders
on vitriol: "You needn't let that slightly funny feeling you have from time to
time about exploitation, oppression, domination develop into full-fledged
unease, discomfort; you could ruin your holiday" (113). She eventually loses
her twisted sense of playfulness and resorts to flat out insults: "An ugly thing,
that is what you are when you become a tourist, an ugly, empty thing, a stupid thing, a piece of rubbish pausing here and there to gaze at this and taste
that" (116). You can't help but wonder why Kincaid is so mean-spirited, so
aggressive, so angry. In your discomfort, you reduce Kincaid to a caricature
and transform her thoughtful, passionate critique of tourism into the ranting
of yet another Angry Black Woman. By stereotyping Kincaid as angry, you
are able to derail her argument and avoid engaging with the ideas she presents
in favor of critiquing her tone. This reaction demonstrates the very "tourist"
behavior outlined by Kincaid: the prioritization of your feelings and pleasure over the humanity and dignity of a less privileged person. Rather than
grapple with your own discomfort and think critically about your role in per-
petuating oppressive power structures like postcolonial tourism, you prefer to
dehumanize and dismiss the author. After all, you are a tourist. What is the
point of a vacation, if not to facilitate your unending comfort and pleasure?

By casting Kincaid as spiteful, you are able to return to your world of luxury and delight, completely devoid of responsibility or guilt.

To clarify, Kincaid's tone and risky stylistic choices do not ensure rejection by her target audience. Those who claim that Kincaid's unapologetically critical tone is not conducive to educating the reader fundamentally misunderstand the author's intentions. Jamaica Kincaid is not your middle school Social Studies teacher: she is not here to give you a sugarcoated lesson on the history of Antigua or hold your hand and help you cope with your guilt. Instead, Kincaid provides us with an authentic, emotional account of her experience as an Antiguan. In my opinion, this is much more valuable and impactful than a so-called impartial, objective narrative could ever be. By muting readers, Kincaid replicates the experiences of native Antiguans who are effectively silenced for the pleasure of tourists. Kincaid's perceived anger—whether imagined or real—only serves to further inform her audience about the condition of the people of Antigua.

Participating in this education is not necessarily an easy task. However, if you are brave enough to put aside your own discomfort and accept accountability for your privilege—to take the same sort of risk as a reader that Kincaid takes as a writer—you, the tourist, just might learn something.

Work Cited

Kincaid, Jamaica. "A Small Place." *Other Words: A Writer's Reader*. Eds. David Fleming et al. Dubuque: Kendall Hunt, 2009. 111–116. Print.

Adding to the Conversation

Preface

For the unit called "Adding to a Conversation," each student travels even further into a wider public audience by taking part in a larger conversation around a subject or issue that they find meaningful. What appeals to each student, what they find important and meaningful, has so much to do with their own histories and experiences. Students begin with a question, research multiple perspectives on the larger conversation around their question, and then imagine a potential audience that ought to hear more about it. Finding a point of entry where they can contribute meaningfully to this dialogue, students then write essays for a specific and more public audience—essays that include representation of and responses to sources but that are ultimately guided by the student's purpose. Here are essays that move beyond the "academic" world.

These essays are evidence of how writing serves the community. In the following essays, the writers bring their perspectives into the "world" and make their voices integral to larger conversations.

We the Media

PETER ANTONUCCI

Antonucci examines the selectivity and bias present in the way American media presents the news. He critiques our wide acceptance of first-world narratives and Western-centric media stories by using a vocabulary that implicates the reader and asks them to take action. His personal reflection, passionate voice, and clear sense of exigency, balanced with outside sources, enlivens our expectations of what a "research paper" is "allowed" to do.

On November 13th, 2015, the world followed Paris through the most violent attack that Europe has seen since the Madrid bombings of 2004. In a disturbingly organized assault, seven gunmen strapped with suicide vests hit multiple points throughout the city, killing 129 people and injuring 352 others ("Paris Attacks: Hollande Blames Islamic State"). Paris and the world recoiled from the blast. Within an hour of the first shots, every major news network was delivering live updates to hundreds of thousands of attentive viewers around the globe. Coverage continued through the night, and by morning the aftermath was seen not only in the pictures of blast areas but in the French flags projected onto national monuments around the world and overlaid on countless Facebook profile pictures. Now, as France attempts to make some sense of the attacks, the world mourns with it.

The human toll of the Paris attacks and the shock it generated is enormous, yet the attacks also highlight just how rapidly our world media can mobilize to bring attention and sympathy to a crisis. The swift response and the continued support given by the global community showed that in general, we as a human race care very much when innocent people are senselessly murdered—and we desire to mourn with those affected even when they are our neighbors on the other side of the ocean.

Where, then, were the Lebanese flags? The question has been raised often in the wake of recent attacks. French flags have been spread across the world in a beautiful act of solidarity with a people tragically attacked. Not often mentioned, however, is the fact that on November 12th, just one day before the

Paris attacks, two suicide bombers set themselves off in a busy Beirut suburb, killing over forty people and injuring almost two hundred more (Barnard). The world was silent. There were no live updates on the situation. There were no Facebook profile pictures changed to mark the tragedy. Lebanon was left on its own to deal with the worst attack it had experienced in twenty years. We are left to ask why.

At this instant I do not know what is happening in Germany. There is no part of my brain that warns me when people are suffering in Laos or when they are celebrating in Chile. It is beyond my ability as a single human being to keep track of what is happening in even one small part of the world. For this reason we have the media. Now obviously "the media" is a very vague term; there are a lot of news sources out there, large and small, and almost all of them have their own way of approaching world events and selecting what to focus on. For now, however, let's just say "the media" is a combination of whatever non-primary sources we use to bring us news about the world. We trust the media like we trust our eyes. We expect the media to tell us when and where something important is happening, and we hope that it tells us this accurately and without bias. I hope we also can trust that the media brings us coverage of a story proportional to its importance.

It was here that the media failed in the case of Paris and Beirut. The lives of those killed in Beirut were just as important as the lives lost in Paris, yet the latter got countless headlines with entire sidebars and updates while the former got one or two headlines at best. But before we ask why this is, perhaps we need to understand that this case is not an isolated incident, nor is it limited to just acts of terror. In almost all areas of news coverage, from politics to the arts, western countries routinely receive the majority of media coverage while countries deemed as "third world" are ignored. The exceptions to this occur only when western countries have a vested interest in the goings on of "third world countries," and so by relation third world issues become western issues. In 2006, a study on western media coverage of natural disasters was conducted by an international business analysis company called CARMA. The report quite bluntly concluded that "western self-interest is the pre-condition for significant coverage of a humanitarian crisis" (CARMA 5). The study reviewed 2,000 articles selected randomly out of a pool of almost 12,000, all relating to five major humanitarian disasters in the early 2000s: Hurricane Katrina in 2005, Hurricane Stanley in 2005, the Kashmir earthquake in 2005, the Indian Ocean tsunami in 2004, the Darfur crisis in 2003, and the Bam earthquake in 2003. Of the five, Hurricane Katrina, which resulted in the second lowest casualty count, received 50% of the combined coverage. Meanwhile, Hurricane Stanley, which resulted in only slightly fewer deaths than Katrina, received only 2.5% of the coverage (CARMA 17). Similar disparity was seen in all other disasters, leading the report to aptly conclude that "there appears to be no link between the scale of a disaster & media interest in the story" (CARMA 11).

Oddly, however, a strong correlation *was* found between the extent of media coverage and the amount of western political and economic interest in a disaster. For example, when comparing coverage of Katrina and Stanley, the CARMA report highlighted the fact that Katrina could be used to attack the Bush Administration which gave it political weight and, in turn, greater coverage. Stanley, on the other hand, hit Guatemala, and despite a death toll of over a thousand, it had very little impact on the global economy and could not be used as political fodder in anyone's agenda (CARMA 11). The result was virtual silence from the world. The deaths of hundreds were ignored in favor of a more politically active story—a trend that is repeated all too often. Our media is failing to provide coverage of events proportional to their seriousness.

Who makes this call? Who decrees that a man shot dead in suburban America bears the same weight as twenty dead in Syria? Is there a malevolent goon in a high corporate skyscraper somewhere cackling manically as he directs the world's media away from natural disaster victims in Guatemala? "Well that would be us," writes George Saunders. "Who runs the media? Who *is* the media? The best and the brightest among us" (246). Saunders, a well-known writer for magazines such as *The Guardian* and the *New York Times*, addresses the issue of who to blame for inadequate reporting in an essay called "The Braindead Megaphone." The root of the problem, he claims, is that journalists have to write stories that people read. Speaking on the mass media industry he writes:

> To stay in the game one must prove viable; to prove viable, one has to be watched; to be watched one has to be Watchable, and in the news business a convention of Watchability has evolved—a tone, a pace, an unspoken set of acceptable topics and acceptable relations to these topics—that bears, at best, a peripheral relation to the truth. (Saunders 247)

The simple fact Saunders points to is that the media is controlled by what the viewers want to see, not by what is actually happening. If, in general, we want to hear about the election polls, then we click on articles and turn to channels where the election polls are being analyzed. If we don't want to hear about election polls, we don't click on articles or broadcasts talking about them. We change the channel and the media stops reporting on election polls entirely because it doesn't make money. Part of the blame for lack of coverage around non-western tragedies therefore lies in the foundations of consumer-driven media. News agencies are not free to report on whatever they want; they must report on what will be read or watched because that is what makes money. Unfortunately, however, unless journalists and editors and cameramen and everyone involved in the news gathering industry suddenly become willing to work for free, this isn't going to change. The only other place to look for a solution, then, is to ourselves.

We own the media. Every time we decide what channel to watch or what article to click on we determine a very small fraction of what the media focuses on. If the media ignored the attacks in Lebanon in November it is because we've been ignoring Lebanon far longer. The fact that coverage of natural disasters is correlated more with political and economic interest rather than humanitarian cost should disturb us. This seems to say that the amount of time we spend focusing on politics and worrying about money greatly outweighs our basic concern for everything else happening in the world. Surely we have a duty to change this. While there may be no simple solution, we could start by looking outside of our comfort zones. If we spent time actually reading about world events—those that have no effect on us—perhaps we would begin to care. If we then began to act on this care by reading more in depth, by looking for facts and perspectives beyond those that simply appear on our Facebook feeds, perhaps our caring would be turned into real action. It's easy to preach optimistic, happy thoughts on a subject like this, but I am confident that through intentional and direct action a real shift in media focus can be obtained.

There is a problem, however, that should be noted. Inevitably we begin to ask ourselves *why* we should strive to change the media's focus (perhaps in reading this you have already begun to ask this). Doesn't it make sense after all that "western media" should focus on "western stories"? Furthermore, will simply focusing on problems really do any good?

As for the first question, we must simply realize that the divide between the western world and third world is a complete illusion. In an increasingly connected world, local issues have a way of crossing borders and becoming global issues. If we in the West ignore issues until they become relevant to us and then suddenly choose to act, we end up blindly attacking problems, ignorant of their background (e.g., the invasion of Iraq). Furthermore, and far more importantly, should it really matter to us what nationality the victim of a tragedy is? We find it natural to care about those similar to ourselves, geographically and culturally, but we should never do this at the expense of ignoring those we cannot easily relate to. Instead, for the sake of love, we should put in extra effort to reach out to those who are distant from us.

The second question remains, however. Will simply caring more about the rest of the world change anything? The answer is likely no. Tears have never stopped genocides or plagues or acts of terror. But in expressing sympathy, even our sympathy for something that is happening a world away, we do take the first steps towards real peace. I do not believe that we can fix any of the world's problems on our own. There will always be wars and rumors of wars, but in first mourning tragedies, and then making even the slightest effort to fix them, we are crying out for true justice.

Works Cited

"Paris Attacks: Hollande Blames Islamic State for 'act of war.'" *BBC News*. BBC, 14 Nov. 2015. Web. 18 Nov. 2015.

Barnard, Anne. "Beirut, Also the Site of Deadly Attacks, Feels Forgotten." *The New York Times*. The New York Times, 15 Nov. 2015. Web. 20 Nov. 2015.

CARMA International. "The CARMA Report on Western media coverage of Humanitarian Disasters." *Imaging-Famine.net*. CARMA International, Jan. 2006: 1–17. Web. 20 Nov. 2015.

Saunders, George. "The Braindead Megaphone." *Other Words: A Writers Reader*. Eds. David Fleming et al. Dubuque: Kendall Hunt, 2009. 239–248. Print.

We Are the 42%

ZACHARY A. CORRIVEAU

In a deft political analysis, Corriveau reaches back into a moment in history he believes the U.S. may be ripe to reproduce in the 2016 presidential election. In a conversational tone, he carefully analyzes how Theodore Roosevelt's second-place finish in the 1912 presidential campaign demonstrates that an independent can profoundly affect the outcome of a national election. By posing rhetorical questions and delaying disclosure of key details, Corriveau creates tension and interest in his argument.

S.1982, also known as the Comprehensive Veterans Health and Benefits and Military Retirement Pay Restoration Act of 2014, was introduced to the Second Session of the Senate of the 113th United States Congress on the 2nd of February 2014, and, like every other piece of legislation introduced in the U.S. political system, no one cared. All right, some people cared (like the senators who were debating it, one would hope), but the majority of the United States population—the young, the old, the Democrats and the Republicans—didn't even know it existed. But still, twenty-five days later, S.1982 was brought to the floor of the Senate, and the one hundred men and women who represent the country decided by a majority vote that this bill was not fit to be a law. With just four votes shy of the total sixty it needed to leave the Senate, it wasn't a total failure. It was wholly supported by fifty-three of the fifty-four Democrats (one didn't vote) and two of forty-five Republicans (with two not voting) ("Senate Blocks Democrats' Bill"). But it was at that precise moment that everyone (well, most everyone), took their heads out of the sand and started caring. Why? The bill was not a radical policy changer, and the idea of it was generally well received. No, it was the "who?" and the "why?" that surrounded S.1982 that woke people up.

Despite being known for representing an image of traditionalism, family values, and the "defense of Western Civilization from the challenges of modernist culture and totalitarian governments" (Schneider xii), the Republican Party made an eyebrow-raising move with S.1982. They went against their largest demographic—war veterans—because of the people and the policies behind the bill. The bill would have given financial aid to veterans from unused portions of money for overseas military actions that had been cut short. "I... have a hard time understanding how anyone could vote for tax breaks for billionaires, for millionaires, for large corporations and then say we don't have the resources to protect our veterans" said the creator of the bill, Sen. Bernie Sanders (qtd. in "Senate Blocks Democrats' Bill"). Yes, you read that right: one of congress's two independent congressmen sponsored a bill that could have been easily accepted by both liberals and conservatives. Yet by the end of the day, S.1982 was rejected and numerous changes had been tacked onto it, including unexpected and drastic sanctions against Iran. This is not the first time in history when two parties butted heads and an independent stepped into the spotlight. In fact, something very similar happened just over one hundred years ago.

The year was 1912, and just like every four years since the founding of the country, there was a presidential election. While it really isn't talked about much today, it certainly brings up an interesting point concerning parties, elections, and a split in public policy. What makes this election really interesting? There were four candidates. Republicans supported the incumbent William Taft, Democrats supported Woodrow Wilson, and Socialist Party candidate Eugene Debs ran as well. But most surprising was that former President Theodore Roosevelt ran again under a new, independent Progressive Party since he had failed to be backed by his former Republican party. After an intense campaign, the ever popular Roosevelt made a surprise finish, raking in 27% of the popular vote, beating Taft, who would only get 21%. Roosevelt effectively split the voters of the entire Republican Party, so the final winner was Wilson, with only 42% of the popular vote (Avlon). This would be the only time in history where an independent party would come in second. The reason for this? At the time, there was a huge divide in the political minds of the Republicans. As John Avlon, a political columnist, explains:

> The [Progressive] party's platform backed giving women the right to vote, the abolition of child labor, minimum wages, social security, public health standards, wildlife conservation, workman's compensation, insurance against sickness and unemployment, lobbying reform, campaign finance reform and election reform.

Some of those ideals even trickled down through the century, especially children's labor laws and social security. The more conservative side of the Republicans wanted high import taxes and a decline in unions, and generally stuck to the party line. Thus, a huge rift in the party formed, and caused the Democratic Party to win, even though they easily could have lost if the Republican Party was whole. While this result wasn't the best for the new independent party, it made quite a statement: a third party in a two party system can make an impact with the right platform and the right leaders.

So what could the failed veteran's bill and the election of 1912 possibly have to do with each other? When looked at alone, not much. But the failure of S.1982 is only the most recent episode in a series of extreme political divides that have built up between the two parties over the last decade and have continued to spiral out of control. The end result is a lack of legislative execution and a rapid increase of disgrace for the entire system. Looking back over the past six months, there have been countless times where the split houses of Congress have failed to get anything done: a national budget, gun control, women's rights, increasing the debt ceiling, nationalizing healthcare, and the largest of them all—a culmination of all of these—a total government shutdown for three weeks. This is the very definition of a government system not working. In fact, congressional approval was at its lowest ever at 9% (Newport), although it has increased to 13% in the following months. The reason for this? The 113th Congress has also been one of the least productive Congresses ever, with only 56 bills passed in the entire year (Little). The year before a whopping 231 were passed, and that was still considered incredibly few. Before that the lowest was in 1995, with only 333. The lowest year to ever get close to that was back in 1948, when Truman had the "Do Nothing" Congress that only passed 906 bills (Little). So in 2014, S.1982 isn't the only thing our Congress can't agree on. No matter whose party you may side with, it has become pretty apparent that our Congress has not done its job.

But if this has been going on for decades, is there anything current that indicates a change? Yes, you could say that. In January 2014, a new Gallup Poll survey found something that seemed impossible: "42% of Americans, on average, identified as political independents in 2013" (Jones). Even since this survey was started in 1988 (see Figure 1), there has been a sharp rise in voters who identify with neither party, enough to outrank the other two parties on their own. This is absolutely outstanding. How can a nation have such a divided government when its people don't fully support either side?

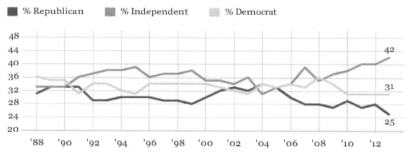

Party Identification, Yearly Averages, 1988-2013

■ % Republican   ■ % Independent   ■ % Democrat

Based on multiple day polls conducted by telephone

Figure 1.

Yet Independents have largely been shunned in this country. Almost always associated with throwing a vote away, they never seem to gain traction like the two main parties and usually appeal to extremes on one side or the other. But with the high disapproval for Congress and the Gallup poll, could there be a chance? Like in 1912, the split in opinion could open up a spot for a 2016 independent, and the Senator from Vermont could very well fill it. Yes, the same one who introduced S.1982. In March 2014, Bernie Sanders announced, informally, that he would be prepared to run for President of the United States (Nichols). And while he was initially adamant that he was not officially beginning a campaign that early on, he is now a clear contender in the 2016 presidential race. In a way that is reminiscent of Roosevelt in 1912, Sanders has had a track record for standing out. Openly attacking economic and social wrongs, implanting more social policies, and proving himself a man of the people, Sanders could be the man for the job. There is certainly an atmosphere for it.

Works Cited

Avlon, John. "What We in 2012 Can Learn from Teddy Roosevelt in 1912." CNN. Cable News Network, Aug. 2012. Web. 8 Apr. 2014.

Jones, Jeffrey M. "Record-High 42% of Americans Identify as Independents." Gallup, 8 Jan. 2014. Web. 7 Apr. 2014.

Little, Morgan. "Congress Set to Pass Historically Few Laws in 2013." *Los Angeles Times*, 11 Dec. 2013. Web. 8 Apr. 2014.

Newport, Frank. "Congress Job Approval Drops to All-Time Low for 2013." Gallup, 10 Dec. 2013. Web. 8 Apr. 2014.

Nichols, John. "Bernie Sanders: 'I Am Prepared to Run for President of the United States.'" *The Nation*, 6 Mar. 2014. Web. 8 Apr. 2014.

"Senate Blocks Democrats' Bill Boosting Veterans' Benefits." NOLA.com. The Associated Press, 27 Feb. 2014. Web. 8 Apr. 2014.

Schneider, Gregory L. *The Conservative Century: From Reaction to Revolution.* Lanham: Rowman & Littlefield, 2009. Print.

Silent Spectator Seeking Solutions in the South Shore

DANIELLE FAHEY

From the beginning, Danielle Fahey's personal anecdote about watching friends smoke high doses of Oxycodone grabs you and refuses to let go. Her essay incorporates personal interviews, news articles, and drug statistics in order to understand the rise in drug abuse on the South Shore. Fahey ends with a deeper understanding of the issue than when she began, and leaves her readers with the responsibility of not remaining silent witnesses to this growing abuse.

As I sat on a friend's couch watching *Family Guy*, I could hear the boys whispering behind me. They were being strange—sketchy even—so I turned around and looked over at them; the conversation stopped. As I asked, "What are you guys talking about?" Pat* walked over and sat beside me. "Fahey," he started, "I know I can trust you, and you're the shit and one of the coolest people I know, so please don't freak out or anything, but we're about to smoke some jams." I froze. They were smoking Percocet 30s, prescription pain relievers similar to Oxycodone. "Why?" I inquired. "I don't know," he chuckled, "because we want to. Don't worry. It's not a big deal. You're cool. Don't say anything to anyone, though." The boys came and sat down around me and began folding up squares of tinfoil and crushing the small blue pills onto them. As they began lighting the bottoms of the foil, a scent of marshmallow filled the air. I scrolled through my phone trying to distract my eyes from the scene unfolding in front of me, but it was odd, the whole situation—I was sitting in a room with a group of close friends as they smoked prescription pills to get high. Essentially, I was watching them begin to throw their lives and futures away, but I was silent. Maybe it was because the smell wasn't worrisome, or maybe because they weren't using needles and spoons, or maybe I was just too scared to say something, but I sat there quietly and patiently, waiting for them to finish and continue on with the night.

"All right, let's play X-Box," muttered Pat. I was relieved that it was over and that things could go back to normal. But when I looked around the room

---

* Names have been changed to protect the identities of participants

and saw their eyes glazed over and their bodies lying lifelessly on the chairs, I realized it wasn't. I stayed for a half-hour longer in that little room, the only sound coming from the NHL game and a couple of mumbled conversations. I saw John passed out, sitting up in his seat, and it looked like the other three were about to do the same. As I shut the door and said bye, no one replied. There were no hugs, no "daps," no goodnights—only four bodies, motionless and mute, high off the drug.

Well-kept lawns, ranch-style houses, and dirt roads that lead to a lake don't exactly scream "Drug Abuse Danger Zone!" But despite the deceiving looks of innocence and unobtrusiveness, the small towns of south shore Massachusetts have been hotbeds for prescription pill and heroin abuse for the past few years. It's difficult to believe these "bedroom communities once considered immune to such problems" (Schiavone) have been the locations for over one hundred opiate related deaths in just a few years. "In 2009 and 2010, 31 men and women died of an overdose in those 10 towns [Abington, Hull, Cohasset, Hanover, Hingham, Marshfield, Pembroke, Scituate, Norwell, and Rockland]. That is one person every 23 days" (Schiavone). In addition, the neighboring towns of Weymouth, Quincy, and Braintree had 91 deaths in that same two-year period; that is one death every 8 days (Schiavone). Things have only worsened since 2010, and I haven't seen signs of it slowing down. It's possible that at fifteen, I wasn't old enough to know abusers, but it's also possible that the regularity of knowing an addict has increased. These numbers are alarming, but the stories and struggles of each number, each person, are what is even sadder and more difficult to understand.

In a study conducted by Alfred Lindesmith, it was found that many abusers began using heroin when in a group of already abusing peers (qtd. in Inciardi 99). I found this to be true when interviewing a friend, Nick Gormley, about his heroin addiction:

> I did it basically because the kids I started hanging out with (class of 2011) were doing them [prescription pills] at the time…and that's generally how everyone starts. They're hanging out with people who are doing them and think they are bigger and stronger than the drug and think they can do it for fun here and there and not get addicted.

It's scary to think about this in relation to the epidemic on the south shore, where illicit drug abuse in the past month, as well as the rate of drug induced deaths and treatment admission exceeds the national average (U.S. National Office of Drug Control). With the drugs so easily accessible and with so many users, it's worrisome that the chances of being put into a situation like Gormley describes, or having someone you know put in such a situation, are very real, and frankly, quite likely. I am a talented athlete, successful student, and a hard worker—I am far from the stereotypical image of someone who is surrounded by drugs. But many abusers are far from the image too; my friends didn't look like the kinds of kids who would snort dope, but it turned out that they were. In an article posted by the *Patriot Ledger*, the backgrounds of five local overdoses are described: "One was a 24-year-old nursing student from Hull. Others were a 41-year-old carpenter from Hingham, a 41-year-old fisherman from Scituate, a 49-year-old real estate developer from Hanover, an 18-year-old student from Norwell" (Schiavone). Heroin "does not discriminate on the basis of age, sex or lot in life" (Encarnacao).

It seems that addiction is something that happens subconsciously, often without warning or much notice. Users start off trying the drug "just once" but suddenly they are getting high daily. No one *thinks* that it's going to happen, and they certainly didn't plan on it. It is simply something that just *happens*. Inciardi bluntly states, "Users typically think that addiction will not happen to them" (99). But what happens when it does? One study found that addicts were more likely to abuse as they became stressed out or unhappy. Also, they found that when an addict heard, saw, or discussed the drug, their addiction was triggered (Preston and Epstein 29). As I interviewed a friend who has battled with his opiate addiction for some time now, I asked why he kept using the drug, even after reaching one of the lowest points of his life. Mike answered:

> I'd cry my eyes out randomly because of how badly I get depressed when I'm not using it. I was going strong [without heroin] when I saw a commercial about addiction, and it put getting high in my head. I thought, eh I'll only do it once, knowing damn well what would happen, and when I woke up after getting high, feeling not dope sick but disgusted with myself, I got high again to take away the pain, even though the better choice would be to accept the fact I messed up and move on.

"Why people use heroin, or any illicit drug for that matter, is not altogether understood" (Inciardi 99). In fact, it is something I do not understand at all.

As an onlooker and a friend, I have become increasingly concerned about the problem occurring right in my hometown. I know many users are tempted to try it because of the drug's sensations and the feeling of euphoria that they become addicted to, and I know peer pressure is an influence in testing it out. Once someone is addicted, I know there is not only a psychological addiction, but a physical one too. I know a battle with a heroin addiction is not an easy one, and I am thankful every day for my strong will to never sample it. But what I don't know is how can we prevent it?

I suppose if the answer to that question were so easy, there would be no such thing as addiction, and the psychologist who found the answer would be vacationing somewhere in Turks and Caicos. However, I feel there must be *something* we can do. Can we educate our peers on the dangers and effects of the drugs? Can we make an example of full-blown addicts and show how their lives have digressed? Can we realize that each person who has overdosed, each number in those statistics, is different and may need different treatments? Also, how can we prevent something that is so well disguised behind nice public schools and lovely cul-de-sacs? When I began writing this paper, I thought that I may have known a solution to the problem. However, through interviews and research, I have found that there is a lot more that goes into a heroin addiction than just weak willpower and a needle. In fact, I may have only found that there may never be an exact solution to something so complex and unruly.

I have learned one thing though: if you are sitting in a room where you know something bad is about to unfold, do not divert your eyes, do not silence your voice. Simply use reverse peer pressure, calmly and kindly, and remind those around you of what they are about to do to their lives and the lives of their friends and families; you may save their lives, or at least not let these drugs claim another victim. At the end of our interview, Mike told me, "I feel like a prisoner to this shit," and that is not a way you want a friend to feel.

Works Cited

Encarnacao, Jack. "Death Certificates Tell Story of Complex South Shore Overdose Epidemic." *Patriot Ledger.* Patriot Ledger, 20 Feb. 2012. Web. 6 Nov. 2013.

Gormley, Nick. Message to Danielle Fahey's iPhone. 5 Nov. 2013. Text Message.

Inciardi, James A. *The War on Drugs IV: The Continuing Saga of the Mysteries and Miseries of Intoxication, Addiction, Crime, and Public Policy.* Boston, MA: Pearson/Allyn and Bacon, 2008. 89–113. Print.

Nelson, Mike. Message to Danielle Fahey's iPhone. 5 Nov. 2013. Text Message.

Preston, Kenzie, and David Epstein. "Stress in the Daily Lives of Cocaine and Heroin Users: Relationship to Mood, Craving, Relapse Triggers, and Cocaine Use." *Psychopharmacology* 218.1 (2011): 29–37. *Academic Search Premier.* Web. 6 Nov. 2013.

Schiavone, Christian. "Small Towns on South Shore Not Immune to Drug Deaths." *Patriot Ledger.* Patriot Ledger, 25 June 2012. Web. 31 Oct. 2013.

United States Office of National Drug Control Policy. *Massachusetts Drug Control Update.* US Office of National Drug Control Policy, n.d. Web. 6 Nov. 2013.

Where Does Our Data Go?

JEREMY KELLEHER

Jeremy Kelleher opens his essay with an anecdote that explains how those annoying pop-ups on the Internet just happen to focus on our preferred brand of casual shoes. We know that using computers compromises our privacy, but Kelleher brings the extent of the problem to our attention. By performing a painstaking analysis of the privacy policies of the Internet's two biggest players—Apple and Google—he shows the huge disparity in how each company manages our data and informs us of the choices we have available to us as Internet users.

Did you ever wonder how Google curates the perfect advertisements targeted solely at you? In order to recommend the latest Crocs on your sidebar, Google has to first know a little bit about you as person. Google starts by using your most recent search terms, noting that you are interested in colorful, cheap clothing. Next, Google will analyze your status updates describing your countless beach trips, noting that you probably like shoes that breathe. Then, Google will check your search history, recording that you haven't bought new flip-flops online in over a year. Finally, they'll take this information they've collected about your feet, sell it to the highest bidding, casual-footwear-selling company (Crocs) and allow them to post an advertisement on your browser, recommending their product.

This idea is what is known as "Big Data." Big Data is the term for databases full of an individual's personal information, categorized to produce trends and statistics, and it is very valuable to large companies that sell goods ("What Is Big Data?"). Because it is so valuable, some companies sell their databases of your information to other companies, thereby turning you, as a user, into a product. Different companies handle our data in different ways, and they all fall somewhere on a data-privacy continuum, with polar-extremes at full privacy and none whatsoever. It is up to us, the users, to become informed about where the companies we use fall on this spectrum. If we aren't aware, we are forfeiting our right to information privacy, allowing every picture of ourselves in Crocs to become available to any company with enough money to buy them.

How do we choose which services are going to secure our data? In an article published in *The Information Management Journal*, Julie Gable, president of a firm that specializes in electronic data management, discusses the basic requirements of any company's security system. She notes that a service must have formally written privacy policies and must abide by those policies in all cases. In terms of selling users' personal data, Gable demands that each company "discloses personal information to third parties only for the purposes identified in the [privacy policy] and with the implicit or explicit consent of the individual" (39). What this means for users is that all of the information regarding where our information is going is in the privacy policies we are clicking over. We are all guilty of scrolling to the bottom of privacy policies and blindly agreeing, but it is important to at least note what companies are doing with the data we provide to them. Most companies include short summaries of their privacy policies in the "About Us" section of their Websites, and this can provide you with all the information you need. When choosing online services, we all need to know more about where our data is ending up, and in doing so, we can contextualize that service on our privacy spectrum. If you don't know where a company falls on the data-privacy spectrum, you should not be using their services.

Now that we know to check for a privacy policy, let's take a closer look at what types of services exist today. The two main competitors in the digital cloud space are Apple and Google, and they each take different approaches in securing their respective user's data and privacy while also abiding by Gable's rules of disclosure. These two services provide context for what this data-privacy spectrum looks like.

Apple takes a locked-down approach by ensuring their users that none of their data will be sold to third-party companies or organizations for the basis of advertising. In their "Privacy Policy," Apple dictates that "personal information will only be shared by Apple to ... improve [their] products ... it will not be shared with third parties for [their] marketing purposes." This means that while some personal information will leave Apple's servers, it will only be used for features that the user allows (e.g., sharing a location when a user requests to know her local weather). Moreover, Apple takes precautions when sending this data: "Siri and Dictation do not associate this information with your Apple ID, but rather with your device through a random identifier." When Apple sends your data (in this case voice recordings) to their own or outside servers, they send a random string of characters to identify your device so that your data is not traced back to your personal identity. Tim Cook, Apple's CEO, summarizes the company's privacy policy saying, "we have ... never allowed access to our servers. And we never will" ("Apple Privacy Policy").

Apple's servers are not open for third party use, which places them on the private-data side of our spectrum.

Apple's strategy, while locked-down, does not allow for features based on the personal content they've collected, like recommendations based on your search history or voice-recognition. Google takes a more open approach to user security and data privacy in order to give its users the more personalized features mentioned above. In one section of its privacy policy, Google illustrates the methods it takes to find your location, saying, "we may use [your] IP address to identify your general location … we may infer your location from your search queries" ("Google Privacy Policy"). After using this information (whether it be location information or other personal data), Google builds a database of information to provide personalized content for each one of its users. Google then shares the data you've provided with other companies when you allow it to do so. The privacy policy says "Google will share personal information with companies, organizations or individuals outside of Google when we have your consent to do so" ("Google Privacy Policy"). Based on the big data it has aggregated, Google shares/sells users' information to other companies, but it does this for the purpose of offering personalized content to its users (i.e. targeted advertisements, simple-sign-in with one user account, etc.). This is the main software scheme that enables far-reaching personalized features for Google's users, and it is paid for by selling our data. This places Google at the opposite end of Apple on our spectrum, closer to the data sharing side.

These two companies, Apple and Google, lie at either side of our data privacy spectrum. While one maintains the secrecy of the user's personal identity at the loss of personalized content, the other unmasks the source of the data, revealing the user's true identity to third-party companies for tailoring content specific to that user. These two companies can provide the framework for what companies exist currently in the technological sphere, but they do not fully exemplify the practices of every company. Use these companies as comparisons in researching privacy policies so that you can understand if a certain company's policy is right for you.

As users, we deserve to know where our data is ending up because, after all, it is our home addresses and photos that are being bounced across companies' servers like a ping-pong ball. Do you know who has access to your home address or those pictures of you at the beach? If the answer is no, then don't blame Google for being "creepy" when you get an ad for Crocs on your sidebar. It is no one's fault but your own for not understanding your data's itinerary once it leaves your computer.

Works Cited

"Apple Privacy Policy." *Apple*. Apple Inc, n.d. Web. 9 Nov. 2014.

Gable, Julie. "Principles For Protecting Information Privacy." *Information Management Journal* 48.5 (2014): 38–42. *Academic Search Premier*. Web. 22 Oct. 2014.

"Google Privacy & Terms." *Google*. Google. Web. 9 Nov. 2014.

"What Is Big Data?" *Business Analytics and Business Intelligence Software*. SAS The Power to Know. Web. 7 Nov. 2014.

Building a Community on Two Wheels

RACHAEL LYONS

Lyons draws her reader into a conversation about environmental issues facing the U.S. by opening her paper with a delightfully descriptive anecdote about her morning run on the sparsely populated Norwottuck bike path. By situating her topic in a relatable, local context, Lyons illustrates how a broad topic of global concern can be fruitfully discussed in a short paper.

Six out of seven mornings a week, I wake up between the hours of seven and nine, put on my sneakers, and head to the Norwottuck bike path to get in some miles before class. The first leg of the run takes me from my dorm room to the entrance of the trail. Those initial one and a half miles are spent running past massive parking lots, crossing busy roads, and passing a stream of cars stopped dead in traffic. But then I reach the entrance to the trail. The hustle and bustle vanishes, and I am left alone in the peace of the deserted bike lane. Other than a handful of leisurely cyclists, dog walkers, or fellow joggers, I have the place to myself. To be honest I enjoy the solitude, but as I was running on a particularly beautiful day in October, I couldn't help but wonder why I was the only one taking advantage of the trail. I wondered where people were going and whether they could use the trail to get there, if they *could* use it, why weren't they, and most importantly—if they did, how would that change our community?

We Americans are in denial. Smog is filling up our cities, inequality still plagues the nation, and social justice simply doesn't exist. How do we go about addressing these issues? We must first foster a sense of community. For decades we have been taught that the American dream consists of a 4-bedroom house, a backyard, and a car. We have been taught that having these things and living in suburbia are what it means to be successful. But suburbia has long evolved from being the small, close-knit neighborhoods portrayed in the film *Sandlot*. We suburbanites live on a larger-than-life scale: big houses, big supermarkets, and big cars to get us back and forth. We build our towns and cities to accommodate cars and trucks instead of accommodating ourselves. Living on an inhuman scale, we have become less human and have lost our sense of community. So the question then becomes: how do we cultivate a sense of community that will bring about change and make our cities and towns more pleasant places to live? We need to make things smaller. We need to make things human-sized again so we can start to *feel* more human. And I think we can do it with bicycles.

Amherst has a reputation for being a progressive college town. We have co-ops, farmers markets, and yoga studios. We promote composting and preach sustainability. But as I run on the deserted bike path, I begin to wonder how much we really practice what we preach. As I get in my car later that day to go to Trader Joe's, I wonder how much *I* practice what I preach. But to be fair, it's not all our fault. The number one reason American citizens don't bike is because they feel it is unsafe—and with good reason. In 2012 there were 49,000 cycling accidents and 726 deaths reported in the United States ("Pedestrian and Bicyclist Crash Statistics"). Just last year in Amherst, Hampshire College student Livingston Panburg was riding her bike on College Street when she was hit by a truck and killed (Pfarrer). Safety, I will admit, is the number one reason I invested 250 dollars in a parking pass instead of a bicycle when I arrived at the University of Massachusetts Amherst this fall. Although there is a beautiful bike trail connecting Amherst, Hadley, and Northampton, what do I do when the path ends? I'm not sure I'm brave enough to take on Route Nine on two wheels. Not only that, but when I get to Trader Joe's, where will I park my bike? Are there even bike racks? I've never seen them.

Business Insider recently posted a list of the top 20 most bike-friendly cities in the world. Not one of them was in the United States. So why are more people biking in Europe than in the U.S.? The answer lies in design. European urban planners have carefully designed their cities to enable safe commuting via bicycle. Copenhagen, ranked the second most bikeable city in the world, cleverly designed its bike paths so that they lie to the inside of the area designated for parked cars. This way, "parked cars protect bikers from moving traffic, instead of bikers protecting the parked cars" (*Urbanized*). To make cycling efficient, convenient, and safe, Danes also created a speed limit for their bike lanes, as well as stoplights and air pump stations. They even have trash cans along the cycling lanes angled towards bikers so they can dispose of their garbage without having to stop peddling. Small yet innovative changes such as these are imperative in encouraging biking in communities like ours. Having one safe bike trail is a great start, but it is isolated from the places we really need to go—supermarkets, pharmacies, doctors' offices, etc. Unconnected as it is to our everyday destinations, the bike path is considered a recreational luxury rather than a functional commuter roadway. In order to make these bike lanes more appealing for practical use, we need to demand our cities' planners adapt our infrastructure to increase the connectivity of the bike paths while maintaining their safety and efficiency.

Amsterdam, ranked the most bikeable city in the world, illustrates some of the many social benefits that come along with a mainstream, urban biking culture. An article by Gilderbloom et al. compares the United States with the Netherlands on a variety of health, social, and environmental issues. On average, Dutch citizens were mentally and physically healthier than Americans. Crime rates, drug use, and carbon emissions were also much lower on average in the Netherlands than in the United States (Gilderbloom et al.). The connections between health and sustainability and bicycling are obvious. But could the bike-friendly community in Amsterdam also account for its healthier social environment? I think it could. According to the article, "an average biking culture can increase the lifespan of a person 2–4 years… Moreover, the state saves on health-cost payouts because people are healthier" (John Pucher qtd. in Gilderbloom et al.). Physically healthier citizens mean emotionally healthier citizens, which conceivably could lead to lower drug use and crime rates. The same concepts could apply here in Amherst if only given the chance. Changing our roads to accommodate cyclists would be expensive, but in the long term, it could mean major savings in health costs. Some cities in the United States have already begun to create bike lanes and are reaping the benefits. After the opening of a bike path in Leadville, Colorado, the town enjoyed a 19% increase in sales tax revenue ("Economic Benefits of Bicycling"). Money saved in health costs and money made in sales tax revenues would better Amherst's local economy and could be reinvested in the town's educational and philanthropic systems to further benefit the social health of the community. Overall, the creation of bike paths in Amherst could lead to economic, health, and environmental benefits that together would make our town a safer, more pleasant place to reside.

A mainstream biking community can also help foster equality. If the majority of a population commutes by bike, that means CEOs, lawyers, and doctors are riding along side blue-collar workers (Anderson). Biking reduces the social stratification that can be enhanced through car ownership. Cycling also gives mobility to those who are unable to afford cars. In a bikeable/walkable community, lower income citizens also have a more equal opportunity to seek out jobs when compared with their higher-income counterparts. Additionally, the positive environmental changes that biking encourages also have social implications. While wealthier people enjoy the economic means to avoid harmfully polluted urban areas, poorer groups are often forced to occupy these heavily contaminated environments and suffer the consequences. Biking helps reduce carbon emissions and pollution, making our cities cleaner, healthier places to live. A more equal society is one that is democratically healthier and can more effectively lobby for meaningful social change.

Okay, so the argument for creating a more bike-friendly community is pretty clear. Who is against a cleaner, safer, healthier, more equal city? I don't think we are going to encounter much opposition, especially in a place that has a reputation of being full of asparagus-growing hippy farmers. In fact, through my research, I'm finding that a lot of people are already talking about bikes in the Pioneer Valley. In 2010, the University of Massachusetts Amherst created a bike share program in which students, faculty, and staff could rent a bike for 24 hours absolutely free. I also came across a group called "Transition Amherst" whose mission statement is to foster a "vibrant and resilient community—in the face of rising energy-prices, climate change, and economic instability." Obviously, these folks are pro-bike. They put on myriad workshops promoting bicycle commuting, teaching bicycle repair, and educating bikers about how to prepare for cold weather cycling. They even have a class on how to build your own bike trailer!

The town of Amherst is also getting in on the pro-bike movement. In 2012, Amherst celebrated bike week in May by hosting a different event to promote cycling every day of that week, including free breakfast for commuting cyclists and a bicycling rodeo for children that taught safe biking practices. This is all great. But my question is, if all these awesome events are happening to promote a cycling culture, why is the bike trail still empty? Clearly we are doing something wrong.

It is wonderful that we have bike week and bike workshops and bike rodeos. These events are a great start. After all, we need to prove there is cycling interest in Amherst and encourage it to grow. But I think, at least to some extent, we are barking up the wrong tree. If we want to really build a mainstream biking culture in Amherst, we as citizens need to start demanding our authority figures to make Amherst a better place to bike. We need to demand wider, more continuous bike lanes and bike racks. We need to create a bike share program open to the community. We need to make biking safe and accessible so people will actually do it. Although it may seem like there are more important issues than making our streets and parking lots bike-friendly and safe, building a strong biking culture would be an invaluable asset to our community. Bike lanes would allow us to live more sustainably and healthily, and they would begin to promote social change in our community. So let's put our money where our mouths are and start investing in cycling—let's live up to the earth-loving hippy reputation that we love to boast about.

Works Cited

Anderson, Michael. "How Protected Bike Lanes Helped Denmark Win Its War on Inequality." *PeopleForBikes*. Green Lane Projects, 7 Aug. 2014. Web. 21 Oct. 2014.

"Building Community With Bicycles." *Transition Amherst*. Transition Amherst, n.d. Web. 19 Nov. 2014.

Copenhagenize Design Co. "The 20 Most Bike-Friendly Cities In The World." *Business Insider*. Business Insider, Inc, 29 Apr. 2013. Web. 2 Nov. 2014.

"Economic Benefits of Bicycling in Urban Environments." Marin County Bicycle Coalition, n.d. Web. 8 Nov. 2014.

Gilderbloom, John I., Matthew J. Hanka, and Carrie Beth Lasley. "Amsterdam: Planning And Policy For The Ideal City?" *Local Environment* 14.6 (2009): 473–493. *Academic Search Premier*. Web. 2 Nov. 2014.

Keates, Nancy. "Building a Better Bike Lane." *Wall Street Journal - Eastern Edition*. May 4, 2007: W1, W10. *Academic Search Premier*. Web. 21 Oct. 2014.

"Pedestrian and Bicyclist Crash Statistics." *Pedestrian & Bicycle Information Center*. National Highway Traffic Safety Administration, n.d. Web. 4 Nov. 2014.

Pfarrer, Steve. "Cyclist Killed in Amherst Collision Was Hampshire College Student." *GazetteNet.com*. 27 May 2013. Web. 6 Nov. 2014.

Urbanized. Dir. Gary Hustwit. Perf. Rem Koolhaas, Norman Foster, and Oscar Niemeyer. Swiss Dots, 2011. Netflix.

Writer's Statement

Preface

College Writing ends with a "Writer's Statement," where students review their entire portfolios written for the course and harvest some of the most important insights they have discovered—about writing and about themselves as writers. By analyzing their struggles, their choices, their triumphs, they compare their past learning with their present knowledge in order to illuminate where they will need to go as writers in their futures. Learning to write well is a never-ending process, so this Writer's Statement is, in fact, a beginning that launches the student into the world of academic writing. They consider the various "tools" they have assembled in their writer's "toolbox": revision, responding to writing, reflecting on writing, writing for an audience and context, writing with purposefulness and the consciousness of crafting an idea into extended prose.

These following texts are the result of each student's unique experience of *College Writing*. They range from larger insights about the self and about learning to wonderfully pragmatic advice for any writer. We hope you enjoy reading about these students' journeys through *College Writing*, and the wisdom they gleaned as they worked throughout the course. Their advice and the insights they share serve as inspiration for us all.

Personally

PAT McDONOUGH

Pat McDonough enters College Writing *with low expectations for the course, but he is almost immediately surprised to learn how different its methods and goals are from his past experiences. The rhetorical choices he makes in creating his Writer's Statement illustrate many of the goals of the course, and he helps readers understand both the atmosphere of the class and its assignments using quotes from his own unit essays.*

My name. That is all you know about me, reader. In fact, I am willing to bet that many of you completely ignored my name and just began reading. You don't know what I look like, where I grew up, or what I do when I'm not writing essays. You don't know that as I write this I am lying in bed in my dorm room in my pajamas, listening to Weezer while trying not to wake my roommate. Unfortunately, my name is the least important and least interesting thing about me. In order to keep you, a complete stranger, invested in what I have to say, I must establish my own personal voice through unique language and perhaps a few personal anecdotes.

On the first day of class, I stumbled into the room after everyone else and took a seat in the back. I had taken several writing classes in high school, and this one was not going to be any different, or so I decided. We were going to talk about using more sophisticated language in our essays, and maybe about how to form a persuasive argument. In essence, everything I had been learning about writing since the sixth grade. I had taken this exact class—or a close variation of it—so many times now that I wouldn't need to pay attention. Then, the teacher asked us to take out our laptops.

This, too, I had been expecting. We were going to be asked to write a brief journal entry or "all about me" piece as an icebreaker to get to know everyone. That was when we were told to open Facebook and look up our most recent status update. I obliged, wondering where he was going with this. I would be fine, however, as long as I didn't have to share. I was in a new place, after all, surrounded by people I'd never talked to before, and the status I had selected was somewhat odd. But there was no way that we would be asked to share something like that out loud, and if somebody did, it was not going to be me.

Of course, I was the first person asked. I paused, cringing as I reread the half-sentence spread out over my Facebook page. The fact that I had updated my status about the season finale of my favorite TV show now seemed incredibly nerdy. I took a deep breath, and conjured up as much courage as I could. Loudly, I read, "Dude, Breaking Bad, I'm gonna die." There were a few chuckles from around the room, but nothing as bad as I had thought. The teacher began explaining how we use different terminology and writing styles in different contexts, based on our audience, and that I likely would never have written that status that way if I had known I would be sharing it with the class. Or for that matter, if I was going to talk about the show, say, to my parents. It is important to know your audience and to write to them so they can receive the thought you are presenting for their consideration.

Sharing our work turned out to be a big part of the class. Most of it took the form of peer reviews; we would trade our essays with another member in our group to give and receive feedback. I was truly thankful for these exercises. It gave me a break from looking at my own work and see the same topic through someone else's point of view. Because we swapped essays with the same group of people every time, we were able to get comfortable with each other and give constructive criticism instead of incessantly complimenting each other's writing. Responding to questions such as "How can the essay be extended?" or "What specific areas of the essay did you connect to as a reader?" as part of our peer feedback compelled us to read and respond critically and thoughtfully. But sharing peer feedback was not the only instance of sharing our work with our classmates.

I was a gymnast in high school. Somehow I was allowed to compete in the meets as a freshman, unlike some of my teammates. The first time I competed, I was very nervous. I had been practicing all season and now I finally had a chance to show off what I had worked for all season. I hopped up to the pommel horse and began my routine. About halfway through I missed one of my moves and ended up in the wrong position. Under the pressure of having my team, my parents, my coach, and the judge all watching me, I had messed up. I did the only thing I could: I made up the rest of my routine on the spot. It was quite clear that the judge had noticed my mistake and docked points accordingly, but at least I finished my routine without crying and running out of the gymnasium. Similar occurrences happened over the next four years, but I usually managed to keep my cool and at least finish my routine.

In my *College Writing* class I was faced with my biggest fear: presentations. We would get into our peer groups and be asked to respond to a music video or movie clip, connecting it to a composition concept we had learned, such as specificity of details, or to an essay we were reading, like Sontag's essay on war photography. My group and I would try to use all of the time given to us in order to come up with the best responses we could. Despite all of the preparation, in the beginning of the semester I would occasionally forget what I was going to say and start stammering. But then I would remember gymnastics, and how I would be able to rectify a mistake with a little bit of confidence. I was able to do the same in my presentations, and towards the middle of the semester, with the presentation being a regular feature of my class, I eventually stopped forgetting my thoughts and would not stammer anymore. Presentation and public speaking are skills that will always be very prevalent in the business world, the space I hope to work in when I graduate. So I am lucky to have learned to master them.

We learned skills that were tangible and that we could use beyond our classroom. For example, one assignment involved looking at photographs:

In the photos of Ron Haviv, it is clear that he keeps this in mind when reporting on events. One of his most famous photos is of Guillermo Ford, the former Vice President of Panama. In 1989 Ford was attacked by a hired thug after a rally in his support. The image shows the two men in a standoff, with the attacker brandishing a weapon and Ford drenched in blood. The color of the photo is loud and chaotic, an action shot that calls attention to itself. The attacker's right arm and weapon is blurred in motion, moving in on Ford, who appears to be giving off a rather submissive gesture. The amount of action in the photo is enough to generate a surge of adrenaline, with the viewer wondering what happened.

While helping us observe the relationship between art and journalism, the assignment was also an exercise in articulating analysis. We learned how to figure out the objective of the photographers and what their pictures meant in context. Analysis is a very important ability in real life because it helps us to understand the things that surround us. In order to properly communicate with others, we must be able to understand what they mean. Helping others to understand us is also an important technique, and attention to detail is the best way of doing so. Our first essay had us writing about our homes:

My town is in the middle of a forest. The omnipresent trees made me feel small. After many years, you got used to seeing the changes from the brown and red of the autumn to the bare snow-covered branches of the winter, the small buds in the spring. Being used to these giant beings did not make me comfortable with them, however. They often blotted out the sun, forcing any life that lived below to live in their shadows. The trees held secrets, and during the dead of night on calm summer nights you could hear them whisper to one another. For those few short, hot weeks I could fit in. Gazing over the ocean, with the pungent marsh air pushing my hair up, I found that I could see for miles in any direction.

By using descriptive language and specific detail, I was able to convey my thoughts about my hometown to the reader. Instead of simply telling how I felt, the details allowed me to show my feelings. While the readers might not feel the same way I do about the forest or the beach, the detailed descriptions I gave of each are enough to simulate the same thoughts for them. Specificity and attention to detail can make writing relatable, even if the reader does not agree with every word.

One of the last (and one of the best) assignments in the class involved writing about our favorite genre of music and the artists within that genre. We used both our analytic skills and attention to detail to craft a personal and meaningful piece:

The song that can send me back to 1999 immediately is "The Sidewinder Sleeps Tonite," by R.E.M. It starts off with an upbeat guitar and steady drums, with the lead singer coming in with a falsetto imitation of The Tokens' "The Lion Sleeps Tonight," in what is a clear homage to the track. With those first four notes, I am always catapulted back in time. When I was little, my mother would do what she called "spring cleaning." It was essentially the same as what everyone else calls spring cleaning, except she did it around once a month, the whole year round. Every time she decided to clean the house from top to bottom, she would dig through her CD collection. (My mother is an avid fan of any and all kinds of music. Except gangsta rap.) Half of the time she would pull out R.E.M.'s *Automatic for the People* and pop it into the stereo. Cleaning the house was her way of clearing her head, and the music relieved her stress as well as made the floor-to-ceiling scrub downs less abysmally dull.

Writing about music provided excitement as well as a challenge. We had to find a way to express the emotions we associated with our beloved music. I realized that the only way to accurately portray these songs was to dive in headfirst and show the readers my personal thoughts. By putting myself in the spotlight, sharing stories and feelings, I easily captured the essence of the music that I had been listening to my entire life. While showing how I actually felt was a bit tough at first, it definitely paid off in my writing.

Adrien Brody plays an English teacher in *Detachment*. He points out the perils of constantly consuming visual media. If the images are constantly supplied, we never use our imagination. In order to stir our own imaginations, we must read, he says, for reading enables us to create our own images. We live in a world where the visual constantly surrounds us: iPods we stare at when walking across campus, the video games we play, the TV shows and movies we watch. So this class was a welcome challenge and an important learning experience. The multiple exercises in this class, on specificity of detail, on taking analysis another level deeper, and on responding to non-textual media with a written response helped me not only stir my own imagination but also articulate my imagination while bearing my audience in mind.

My experiences with the class far exceeded my expectations. I will always remember it as my first college course, but it was also more than that. We formed a sort of community in that room, joking around and engaging in the friendly competition between groups. It was the only class I looked forward to every day. I am sad to see it go, but I know that the friends I made and the techniques I learned will stay with me.

~~The~~ My Writing Process

JOSEPH SESTITO

Joseph Sestito's reflections on his experiences in College Writing *opens with a tale many students will relate to: his mastering and holding fast to the formulaic rules of five-paragraph essay writing. But his ideas about writing and the writing process change dramatically when he analyzes an essay in* The Student Writing Anthology *that he admires. From this beginning, his Writer's Statement shows rather than tells throughout, as he artfully charts using various pedagogical features of the class in each unit to reach the powerful writing we now see in his final essay of the course.*

What I knew was the five-paragraph essay. What I knew was how to write to ace standardized tests. All I knew was how to write to achieve an end—a grade, the grace of a class exemption.

I was schooled in the small town of Cohasset, Massachusetts. In 4th grade I scored below average on my writing MCAS and so on the first day of 5th grade, after recess, we the underachievers were led into an empty, chairless classroom where the dank air smelled like old shoes, and thick blinds covered the only escape from the bleak brick walls encasing us. We wore serious faces, along with our thinking caps, and memorized a successful essay's structure: an introduction, a thesis with 3 points elaborated in 3 paragraphs, and then, naturally, a conclusion, which restates the thesis. Due in part to a readily handy structure, and part to my own determination to escape the remedial class, I scored above average on the 5th grade MCAS and never had to find my way back into that chairless room. I now knew the formula to writing.

At least I thought I knew.

Then began college, and with it, English 112. To borrow words from our Unit V prompt, "our oddball teacher came in and it all began." What I knew didn't become irrelevant, no; instead my understanding of what *good writing* meant expanded: I acquired writing tools and learned to write with an audience and a context in mind.

Am I moving too fast and summarizing? Let's rewind and try to stay in scene.

In Unit I of English 112, we had to write about a pivotal place in our lives. I chose to write about my hometown. From peer feedback it became clear that to another pair of eyes, my essay seemed like a factual report of my time in Cohasset rather than the paying of homage I was striving for. Before we began revision, we read *The Student Writing Anthology* essay, "Pages of a Diary Never Written" by Tanner Houle. The essay created emotion, I observed, through sensory details that were not just visual (they were also aural, olfactory, and tactile) and through the manner in which Houle *sequenced* these details as diary entries to non-chronologically build a narrative. Using the technique of pastiche, a literary exercise in imitating another's style, I typed out the following paragraph from Houle's essay:

> Outside, the smell of sweet marinated chicken and tender steak thickened the air with a rich aroma. Someone was clapping in tune to a song. Stray laughter made its way up. An insistent clanking rose from the empty cans and bottles colliding in the bin. Voices started calling out our names. It was time to go (45).

Then, I proceeded to type out a paragraph from my first draft:

> I don't really remember the playdates and birthday parties of my early childhood years, but I remember forming a group of friends in 4th grade. Some of the kids were friends of friends from prior school years, others were new to the small school looking for companions. One was the son of a mom's friend who I bonded with at soccer practice when he accidentally spit Gatorade in my eye.

The revised version, as I imitated Houle's style but kept my voice, looked like this:

> We sat next to each other on an uneven bench after the soccer match. He laughed and spat Gatorade in my eye. Thinking that he had acted maliciously, I loaded my mouth with Gatorade and fired back. Our eyes stung, and we started to cry. We washed them and dried our hands, and for a moment, the whoosh of the dryer, blowing its hot breath on our shirts, filled our silence. His name is Dakota and that day we became friends. We trekked downtown to buy candy. At the time the hike was an adventure. But all did we was walk a circle, down then up. We went on to use bikes, we became a group of friends. The confines of the town became a habit and even when we got our licenses, we circled the streets we once biked.

For our second unit, in order to find my way to interact with Susan Sontag's "Regarding the Pain of Others"—an essay on war photography and its moral implications particularly when historic images are presented without context or narrative—I decided to write about a photograph from the Boston Marathon Bombings.

I described the image in adequate sensory details, assuming a comparative essay was well within my wheelhouse, but the structure, my teacher Mr. Akella suggested, constrained what I was trying to express. He shared with me a Web essay, and because I actively read for structural invention, as I was reading I came up with an idea that I wrote about in the reflective letter to myself—an activity that was a required part of our revision process: I decided that rather than creating a forced continuity between paragraphs, with sentences that served no other purpose but to link one paragraph to another, I would present my ideas separated by a line break. Here's an example:

> On the cover of the *Sports Illustrated* were three police officers in fluorescent green jackets standing over an injured runner in a bright orange pinny, the street behind them choked with smoke. What does the picture convey about the sound of an explosion, the chatter of families who at that moment simply gathered clutching cameras and poster boards to cheer on the runners?

> The photograph, a "posthumous reality," is "the keenest of summations" of the bombing, its purpose being to "serve as totems of causes," but "the illustrative function of photographs leaves opinions, prejudices, fantasies, misinformation untouched" (Sontag 261). Without a narrative that gives the image meaning and weight, it merely "haunt[s] us" (Sontag 263).

I ended my essay with a litany of questions. The pillars of the essay structure I'd learned had, quite literally, crumbled. My structure that kept an audience and subject in mind was integral to the context.

For Unit III, I did something I would have never done six months back: I opened a research essay with an anecdote. By beginning with a setting that my audience identified with—a freshman classroom—and by building on narrative skills I'd learned from Unit I, I gained my audience's attention. The drafting process was the most helpful in this unit; it allowed me to manage the different modes of writing: using both quote and summary instead of relying on the former; bringing in our Unit II skills to engage with the texts that I'd selected as my resources; bringing the resources into my text while retaining my voice as a writer through *active analysis*.

When writing my Unit III and Unit IV papers, I saw how *active analysis* draws connections that are not obvious—connections within a text, between, for example, the third and the tenth paragraph, or connections between the text and another text. In drawing these connections I give my voice a presence. Film, music, and social media are also "texts" you respond to, a fitting discovery that book-ended what we'd learned at the beginning of the semester: that we are all writers, and there are a variety of texts we write: from essays to text messages, from grocery lists to emails.

Writing this final paper for 112 made me aware of how internal revision became my writing process. I wrote two drafts for our class, and then, when Mr. Akella invited me to submit my essay to the anthology, I revised it twice more, with some distance between one revision and the other. Earlier, my instinct would have been to submit it right away.

A wise friend once told me the reward of any retrospection is not to speak broadly about having changed—rather it is the opportunity to point to specific shifts, discoveries, and breakthroughs undertaken along the road.

Did I just use my conclusion to restate my thesis? Does it count if it is not a five-paragraph essay? Does it count if through narrative and specific analysis I recreated my journey for you? Does it count even if I sign off with questions?

You know the answer. We learned it together over the course of the essay, right?

Works Cited

Houle, Tanner. "Pages from a Diary Never Written." *The Student Writing Anthology: 2013–14*. Eds. Patricia Zukowski and Dierdre Vinyard. Boston: Pearson Learning Solutions, 2013. 43–47. Print.

Sontag, Susan. "Regarding the Pain of Others." *Other Words: A Writer's Reader*. Eds. David Fleming et al. Dubuque: Kendall Hunt, 2009. 257–265. Print.

Case Study 3: Subject, ████████████

COLIN STIEVATER

Marked by distinctive black bars indicating redacted material, the appearance alone of "Case Study 3: Subject, ████████████*" shows that Colin Stievater has broken the conventions of a typical Writer's Statement. Writing in the discourse of a government report or a psychological study, Stievater experiments with not only redacting phrases, but also placing his analysis of his own writing experience into the persona and voice of a detached observer. This detachment lets readers easily situate themselves in his experience and allows Stievater to comment on his own insights, difficulties and accomplishments in a refreshingly forthright way.*

Objective 1: How did ████████████ *make personal sense of each unit in the study and find his voice within?*

Findings: ████████████ believes this case study was one of the most personal that he has participated in. Almost all of the study's topics made him think about deeper ideas than most typical tiered studies. The ways in which he was prompted to do this study were helpful as well. He specifically mentions 'context' and 'lenses' on multiple occasions, saying, "My instructor helped me see the world around me through a lens of my own making, crafted from my personal context, and helped me understand why I saw it that way." Before enrolling in this study, ████████████ hadn't given much thought to his context. The subject assumed that life was the way it was because it was life, and although in the past he understood that the values that he was raised with affected his outlook on the world, he didn't believe that he applied this concept. ████████████████████ To find this personal sense, the subject considered writing about events that happened recently enough to still evoke emotion within him. Our observers recorded him saying at one point: "Writing with emotion is not only easier because the feelings are recent and clearer (so I can write more), but also more genuine and raw, which helps me write more and keeps my ideas focused."

Exhibit A: Trial 1: ████████████████

Subject was prompted to write about a misfortune he had experienced that could possibly have altered his ingrained concepts of life. ████████████ chose to write about a medical emergency that his father experienced three months earlier. ████████████████████████ With such a recent event to draw from, the subject finished the initial task in under two hours. He is quoted as saying "It flowed naturally and with passion. I could focus more on how to tell the story rather than what to tell." █████████ ███ The following is an excerpt written by ████████████ for this task:

> When I pull over to the side of road because I catch a glimpse of red and blue in my rearview mirror, I don't regret leaving late to wherever I might be going. I don't wish I could pull back out and throttle down the road again. I pause, and I say as close to a prayer as I can get for the family of those lying in the back of that ambulance because I've seen the inside and it's not pretty. I've lived to deal with the idea that health can be taken away just as easily as it can be given. ... And I learned that we are not perfect. We break down, and we wear away. And some day we will need help. And until that day, we should grab life by the horns and not worry about the bull underneath. We can, and should, enjoy our moment, knowing that eventually it will pass, but choosing not to dwell on it.

As for the subject's narrative voice, we believe that this also has a lot to do with the emotional side of the experiences that he referred to. ████████████ doesn't have to work hard to keep a consistent voice when the words flow from his knowledge and sentiments towards a topic. We believe that when the subject keeps the writing emotional and raw, his narrative voice is created. ██████ ██ This, however, remains more hypothesis based on observation than fact, given that we don't know what is going on inside the subject's mind.

Objective 2: How did ████████████ *use the community structure of this study to engage with the work of other subjects and improve his writing?*

Findings: Over the course of this study, the subject had a love/hate relationship with the peer editing process. It seemed that he enjoyed reading what other people who participated in the study wrote, and often our observers noticed that this inspired ████████████ to go on productive tangents in his own papers. His opinion is that having a second set of eyes on anything, especially an academic paper, is always helpful. That said, it took ████████████ a lot of time to effectively complete the peer editing process. Similar to his study instructor, the subject found it hard to simply do a cursory analysis of a peer's paper, and ended up spending a disproportionate amount of time reading over other papers and providing comments. (Refer to Exhibit B.) It is also possible that the lengthy responses by the instructor served as models of inspiration for the subject's peer response process. Further study is needed to determine whether this deficiency is isolated to ███████ or if the process as a whole is inefficient.

Microphones hidden around the study location picked up the subject saying,

> Honestly, the time would have been better spent on my own paper, but good feedback on their work is important to me. The brilliant part of this is that while I was spending all that time on their papers, other students were looking over mine. The edits I received were theirs, and because I had so little time to invest in my own paper, the changes I made were mostly revamped versions of suggestions they made. And this is fine, because two brains are better than one. ███████████████████

After three months of observation, the only dissent that we can find in the subject lies in his attitude towards group-led activities in which he had to participate: the previously effective "generative writing" in preparation for a task. He stated that this type of activity was great by itself and helpful in leading to socialization with participants in the study, but ███████ didn't feel like it added anything to his final paper. His study instructor mentioned that he had an ultimate purpose in devising these activities, so the committee recommends that in further studies he makes these points clearer.

Exhibit B: Trial 3: Peer Editing Letter from ███████ to Fellow Subject: November ███████

Hi ███████,

From what I've seen it looks like you've made a lot of progress on this draft. Although I can't speak much on behalf of your topic because I'm not very well versed in it, from what I can tell, your draft is chock-full of solid facts, and I'm going to put faith in you and assume that the subject matter is all logical and the history works out. As for the research side of the paper vs. your own ideas, this piece starts very top heavy (after the intro), with facts and information from other sources. However, this is then balanced out by your own take on the events later on. ███████ ███████████████ And this is where I found the piece to be slightly, slightly confusing. I like how you try to bring up your own ideas about what might have happened, and I get that this must be insanely difficult because it is inherently impossible to figure out what would have happened in the past if things were different. At first I wasn't sure if musing about the past took on the role of independent thought, but the more I considered it, the more I realized that yes, this is what your paper needed in terms of your own ideas. It shows that you spent time thinking about the different possibilities and gave hard thought to the paths history took. This is, however, where I didn't know whether the ideas were your own or from a source. I'm assuming they are from your own experience, but if not, you should really cite the sources to prevent any misunderstanding in your final draft. Overall I really like the direction that this piece is taking. You added detail from last time, and cut back on details that didn't directly support your ideas, and this helped me follow your narrative path. Good luck on your final draft, and I'll see you in class!

Best,

████████████

Conclusion: Over the course of this study, ████████████ improved as both a human being and a writer. We observed measurable changes in his ability to analyze his surroundings, interpret these results, and put them down on paper in a meaningful way. Throughout this three month study, his morale remained high despite his having to complete multiple, high-anxiety activities assigned by his study leader. It is our professional opinion that based on these results, ████████████ has completed the study with favorable results. These results will be useful to us in the future, both when we examine new subjects, and again bring this study under review.

To My Future Self

JACQUELINE WALSH

Jacqueline Walsh casts her Writer's Statement as a letter to her future self ostensibly to remind her of the critical lessons she has learned in College Writing. *But her use of the second person narrative voice not only serves the form she has chosen; it also allows her to speak directly to her readers, inviting them to follow the same advice she gives herself.*

Writing is a part of you. And this part of you is ever changing. Today, you are not the same seventh grade writer who went three pages over the word requirement because you couldn't get your point across clearly and concisely. You are not the freshman in high school who felt pure satisfaction when you discovered that the key to constructing a strong thesis statement was two simple words followed by a question mark: *so what?* You are not the stressed out junior who believed that her exhausted fingers typed out their best essays at eleven o'clock on school nights after grueling basketball workouts. And you are not the excited but anxious *College Writing* student who couldn't seem to project a confident voice through that size twelve Times New Roman font sitting on a glaring white background. But today, you *are* a writer who has learned from each and every set of words you have strung together to form one piece, and you will continue to grow in this way.

Over time, you have established your own set of rules that guide you throughout your writing process. Some of these rules have existed since elementary school, and others have been eliminated entirely as you've matured into a more experienced and knowledgeable writer. My hope is that you always follow these rules that have become second nature to you as you sit down at your desk and pick up a pencil to construct an outline, or as you begin typing the introductory paragraph to an essay. But always remember that adjusting these guidelines is crucial to producing your very best work—because writing is a dynamic skill.

Recall your first *College Writing* experience. You walked in expecting the same type of English class you'd been taking for your whole life, and you had no idea that you would come to see yourself as a writer with a specific style made up of different tones and tendencies, a writer who would use descriptive language as a means of portraying a state of mind:

"It faded along with the last few notes flowing from thin guitar strings—notes whose whisper could barely be heard, and it faded with the stream of silent tears that retrieved my conscience from the blissful place where it was lost" (Unit 4).

You figured you would write in the same way you always had because that's what always worked in the past, but that changed the second you began your first assignment. You were no longer dead set on the fact that your first draft had to be your last because you simply could not move on from a paragraph until it was perfect. You learned that abandoning the strict rules of detaching yourself from writing so as to not include the first person is not only a decision, but also an empowering one where you can more personally and directly address your audience:

"In order to establish our own self-worth without dependence upon our social media accounts for self-assurance, we must allow our online identities to become reflections of ourselves, instead of ourselves becoming reflections of our online identities" (Unit 3).

Confidence finally had a presence in your work because you discovered your voice through strong opinions you worked hard to eloquently present—no matter how black and white or grey those opinions may have been—and for the first time you allowed yourself to be vulnerable as your writing served as a window into your most precious life experiences, experiences that shaped you as an individual:

"But I went in denying myself of my true identity. I boarded the plane as the Absent Girl because I misread my refusal to give up on goals and my ability to lead. I didn't understand that those aspects of my identity are not weaknesses—they are strengths, and they define who I am" (Unit 1).

Above all else, you came to understand that you determine how meaningful your writing can be, and that writing is always a work in progress. With all works in progress, our weaknesses will also play their roles. Sometimes recognizing these parts of ourselves is challenging, but when we can confront our weaker points while using our more established skills to our advantage, the result is always an improvement from the previous attempt. As a freshman in college, you learned that you can be creative with the structure of your writing, and not everything has to be in paragraph format. You learned that you can change the appearance of your words through fonts and spacing, and disrupt the usual patterns you follow to convey your most powerful and emotional points. And you learned that wordiness and over-simplicity of statements, especially introductory statements, lead to vagueness and thus confusion for readers:

"This truth is problematic, as we are led to accept information and stories that are not complete" (Unit 2).

But through more extensive revision and practice with writing more than just one draft, you were allowed both time and distance from your work, which later aided in your recognition of obscure areas in your writing. This step became crucial in expanding upon ideas because it ended up eliminating any ambiguous thoughts that could have complicated your audience's understanding.

As you move on to the next stages of your life, whether that be your last semester of college or your first day at your new career, remember that in a world where communication and interpretation are the keys to establishing who you are, you are always learning. Writing and reading will remain a part of your identity—as outlets for expression, platforms for personal and professional relationships, and methods of comprehension. You are always a student of the environment in which you live, and the lessons you have learned through your journey as an evolving student-writer will appear in Mother's Day cards, thank you letters, e-mails to your boss, and speeches at your brothers' weddings, grandparents' birthday parties, and Mom and Dad's anniversary dinners. As long as you are willing to learn, you will continue to improve, and through your writing you will discover a voice that you never knew you had.

Finding Peace—The Intimate Experience of Writing

PETER WHITE

In his Writer's Statement, Peter White moves between discussing his work on particular assignments and delving into his personal context. He has discovered that the act of writing itself can create for him what he calls "pockets of air" in the midst of an era filled with endless distractions. And these "pockets" allow him to use writing for many purposes: to learn, to discover, to heal, and to face and change uncomfortable facts about himself.

The human mind has a fascinating and mysterious strength in us all. It is the "key" to life that makes us individual from the rest of the world. Through the many powerful feelings and thoughts in each of us, the mind and all that we experience help shape us into who we are. They are a part of our greater story, subconsciously helping make decisions for us every day. However, without a method of channeling, processing, and understanding our thoughts and feelings, we can quickly lose sight of who we are, what our purpose is, and how to become the best we can be. There are many practices to help center the mind, but not all methods work for everyone because each of us is uniquely different from everyone else. For me, I found peace and continue to find peace through writing. What follows is a small telling of the journey I have taken to get where I am today. I have not fully reached my destination, but I have crossed a milestone that has helped me to begin understanding who I am and the many blessings I am privileged to have.

* * *

At the time I was applying to attend a university, I thought college was not for me. I had learned to be a skilled carpenter and have sold the pieces of furniture I make for thousands of dollars. If I really wanted to, I could make a living with my abilities. But during my senior year in high school, I didn't feel ready to commit to college, and I didn't think I would find satisfaction in becoming a furniture maker. I decided to defer my admission and see what the world had to offer me, to see if I could find answers to questions that had plagued me for years. I was a painfully shy individual during my first three years of high school, but I never wanted to be. I felt stuck and questioned my worth even though I had many friends who loved me. Even with my best friends, I would often look at the floor instead of at them as they said hi to me in the halls. In hopes of finding myself, of coming to peace with who I am, I took a job as a full time supervisor to six sub-contractors—a stimulating and multi-faceted job. I was paid handsomely, my work was both efficient and organized, and my supervisor and colleagues welcomed and appreciated me. Despite all of this apparent success, I was still no closer to finding contentment or peace with who I am... until one day I was challenged by a UMass professor to express myself through pen and paper.

* * *

Coming to UMass has been one of the most wonderful challenges I have ever faced, but frankly, there was one challenge I believed I could live without. When I attended New Student Orientation in June before my freshman year and signed up for ENGLWRIT 112, I was very nervous. I had always hated writing, and I knew in my gut that I was going to hate the course. I believed papers were a waste of time, and an entire course dedicated to essay development and revisions would be even more so. But a lot of things happened during this course that proved me wrong. In fact, I have never been more wrong about something in my life.

* * *

I believe that for the majority of people, the most difficult battles we experience in life are the ones we have within ourselves, and it is easy to avoid fighting them in an age where distraction is so readily available. In order to find peace, it is essential for an individual to find a way to overcome these inward battles. We need to find what I think of as "pockets of air" in each day to allow us to process things in our lives rather than to fill them with distractions. I fell victim to this avoidance, and as a result, finding peace with who I am became my greatest conflict yet. Although life at UMass has greatly helped me find my peace, I have found the majority of my peace through writing.

* * *

Beginning with the first unit of my *College Writing* class, I struggled greatly to understand how to talk about myself. It was not something I had ever practiced, and it made me very uncomfortable. In this essay, I relived a moment in time on my Great-grandfather's farm that has influenced me my entire life:

As my Great-grandfather (Bumpa as I called him) was preparing the tractor so I could drive it, a gift for my sixth birthday, he simply asked me what I wanted to do in life. At six years old, I had never really given much thought to this question; I never felt a serious response was necessary at the time. With Bumpa, however, it was different. Although we spent a lot of time together, he was never a man of many words, and when he spoke, it was with intention and purpose. So I thought about the question while he opened up the hood of the tractor to pour diesel into the tank. When he finished, I remember stating with certainty that I wanted to be a worker man like him. This made him laugh out loud and his response was "Then you will be."

I always knew his words "Then you will be" had a great impact on me, but until this assignment, I had never forced myself to truly consider what these words meant to me. I experienced great enlightenment in this unit because it taught me the power writing can have on an individual. Words greatly influence the impact that a story will have on an audience, and word choice needs to change accordingly depending on the intended audience and purpose of the essay. Learning how to "show" a moment, as opposed to "telling" a moment invites the reader to experience the emotions the author has intended to share. I "show" my Great-grandfather in the final product of my essay:

His laugh was thunderous as he caught each of my siblings and me, and his hugs were the same as always: warm, powerful, and comforting. He could throw each of us very high with little effort, and despite my fear of heights, I was okay with him doing so because I trusted him like no one else. His hands were rough and calloused from the continuous turning of the soil in his fields, and his clothes were neat but stained from the dirt and grease acquired whenever he did maintenance on his tractor.

This "shows" my Great-grandfather because from this excerpt, you can interpret a kind, strong, warm, hard-working man. I could have simply "told" the reader all this, but by "showing" him, I have invited the reader to interpret the story on his or her own. The overall experience is more comfortable and effective for the reader, and as the writer, it was my first step into understanding writing as a way of processing my thinking.

* * *

In the second unit, I learned how to analyze and interpret a text. This was also something I was terrible at. In my entire life, I can confidently say I have read fewer than fifty books and for any argumentative essay, I have always fallen asleep before finishing it. That was up until this unit. Through the intimate discussions in class and with my professor in conferences, I came to appreciate the many different ways an essay can be interpreted. I had never considered the idea that everyone reads and interprets essays differently. I now realize that our own context and life stories greatly influence everything we read, say, and do. And so it is incredibly important that we learn how to understand our own individual context as well as attempting to make contact with both the context of the essay's author and our intended audience. This understanding prompted the topic for my second essay when I read "Is Google Making Us Stupid?" by Nicholas Carr. Upon reading his text about technology and how it is affecting our mental abilities, I challenged his idea and took his work a step further by making observations as to how technology is making us numb. My intention was to encourage my readers to allow less distraction into their lives, enabling them to find the "pockets" I previously mentioned.

Peer responses were very helpful to me in Unit Two because they helped teach me how to write a persuasive argument for my audience. My class had many different personalities, and this allowed me to adapt my essay to reach out to as many different people as I was able. Mostly, my revisions came from the questions my peers asked me during conversations I had with them. They would make statements like "I don't fully understand what you mean by this accusation you are making" and "What advice would you give to help people put down their phones?" These sorts of interactions taught me to consider potential questions readers may have from reading my texts and to answer them before they are asked. Accomplishing this, however, will always require a lot of advice from colleagues and a lot of revision if I am to most success-fully deliver my purpose.

* * *

Revision is the most intimate part of writing; it is when the author needs to test his own work and consider new words, styles, ideas, and methods to most efficiently communicate his ideas. Every essay during my course underwent extensive revisions at least twice, for example, my fourth unit. The goal of this unit was to revise a previous essay for a new audience, with a new purpose, form, and voice. I decided to revise my first essay by writing a letter to my Great-grandfather who had passed away over eight years ago. This was a great trial for me. I hadn't spoken to him since I had prayed to him at his funeral. To share my feelings with him in 1200 words or less was difficult, but this required me to consider what I most wanted him to know about me today. If I hadn't revised my initial draft, where I talked about the weather at his funeral, I would have regretted not telling him how the four words "Then you will be" have shaped me into the man I am today. It's amazing the level of impact a moment can have on a person. With that sentence, one of the most influen-tial men I have ever met built the foundation of the work ethic I have today. If I want to accomplish a goal, I will as long as I go into it with an open and persistent mind. Applying these ethics to writing, I feel more accomplished because of my revisions. In order to successfully achieve revision, you must completely open your mind to understand your own work in a new light. You need to become your audience and answer as many questions as you can. It is very difficult for people to relate to one another unless minds are open and accepting of new ideas. For me, revision became a kind of meditation. I was required to unclutter my mind of all the noise that it is so easily filled with, and create a channel for fresh virgin thoughts to flow. Subsequently, revision brought me one step closer to finding peace within myself.

* * *

Writing is a truly intimate experience. It requires a lot of time and patience, but it will never stop helping you if you take the proper steps to nurture and develop it. I came into this course despising writing, and I now leave this course with a love for writing. My advice to you is this: allow yourself to fall victim to this remarkably enlightening process. I challenge you to expand what you learn in this course and to apply it to every aspect of your life. Use writing to explore your ideas; to channel your thoughts and feelings; and to understand your disappointments, your goals, and your identity. We all have our strengths and weaknesses, but it isn't impossible to harvest our weaknesses and make them stronger. Every time I confront my discomforts through writing, I become more comfortable with them. You can never stop growing if you push yourself. Use this course as a milestone to help you achieve greater than your best. It will be challenging and it will require a lot of time, but in the end, I promise, you will find that you are not only a better writer, but also a well-spoken individual with a voice to be heard. I found my peace in writing. You may not, but I know either way you will greatly benefit if you engage in this experience.